COLD WINTER, COLD WAR

COLD WINTER, COLD WAR

ROBERT G. KAISER

STEIN AND DAY/*Publishers*/New York

First published in 1974
Copyright © 1974 by Robert G. Kaiser
Library of Congress Catalog Card No. 73–81794
All rights reserved
Designed by David Miller
Printed in the United States of America
Stein and Day/*Publishers*/Scarborough House, Briarcliff Manor, N. Y. 10510
ISBN 0–8128–1625–0

For H.G.K., H.J.K., and P.M.K.

". . . And then came that awful winter. It is enough to say of it that perhaps its most crushing blows fell on Britain, our chief ally and collaborator, to whom we looked to take the lead in maintaining the eastern Mediterranean and sharing with us the burdens of occupation and defense of Europe . . ."

Dean Acheson

INTRODUCTION

The cold war has dominated more than a generation. Its hostilities, preoccupations, even its jargon are part of us all. It began as the American solution to the problems of postwar Europe, but it quickly evolved into a full-blown crusade. The crusade spawned new weapons, new fears, new slogans and alliances, and eventually the traumatic war in Vietnam—not the sort of memorial most crusaders would like to be remembered by.

These last years of the cold war have produced a great deal of new writing and debate about its first years. Vietnam was persuasive evidence that the crusade had gone awry, and many historians have tried to explain why. Some of them have gone back to the origins of the cold war to find an explanation, arguing that the confrontation between East and West was, from the beginning, the result of skullduggery, conspiracy, or simple stupidity—mostly on the Western side.

This book disputes that view, but it is not an argument with the "revisionist" historians who have blamed the West—essentially, the United States—for causing the cold war. Rather it is a book about politics, a subject the revisionists have largely ignored. The cold war began because of political decisions taken by politicians. The atmosphere of the times, the perceptions of the politicians involved, the course of world events as it appeared then—these were the factors that produced a cold war. I have tried to recreate those factors in this book. If I have succeeded, the beginnings of the cold war should seem less conspiratorial and more reasonable than they might otherwise.

The book is based on the assumption that the real beginning of the cold war was the Truman Doctrine, Harry S. Truman's decision to provide substantial American aid to Greece and Turkey, which he announced with a declaration of support for

9

"free peoples who are resisting attempted subjugation by armed minorities or by outside pressures." The rhetorical declaration is best remembered now, but the practical decision to help Greece and Turkey (because Britain could no longer help them) was the political step which began the cold war. With that step the United States came into Europe to try to balance and contain Soviet power. With that step Britain dropped out of the front rank of world powers, leaving the game to the Soviet Union and the United States.

The Marshall Plan followed directly from the Truman Doctrine, and effectively divided East and West Europe. Of course it is possible to see origins of the confrontation between East and West much sooner than March 1947, when Truman enunciated his doctrine. The failure of the wartime alliance to work in peacetime was evident more than a year before. The hardening attitudes of British and American officials toward the Soviet Union were also perceptible much earlier. These factors were of central importance when a series of coincidences in the winter of 1946–47 brought on the Truman Doctrine. But until the President spoke out that March, announcing America's intention to assume commitments in Europe and the Near East, the cold war had not really begun.

To describe political history, within a nation or among nations, one must describe events that actually happened. The prejudices and opinions of people involved, their theories or intentions often influence the events of political history; but they may have no influence at all. For example, early in 1947, before the Truman Doctrine committed the United States to an active and specific policy, the president and his colleagues could have opted for a fundamentally different foreign policy, one that would have postponed a cold war, or changed its character, or conceivably even avoided it. For many reasons, this was unlikely: political pressures of many kinds and the inclinations of those involved all pointed toward a firm policy to contain Soviet power. But until the Truman Doctrine, those pressures and inclinations could have been overcome if different events had justified a different course.

This is a book about Britain and the United States, but a silent partner, Joseph Stalin, is constantly in the background. There is almost no documentary evidence about postwar Soviet foreign policy. Even if documents were available, they could easily be irrelevant, for Stalin personally made every important decision.

What were Stalin's real ambitions after the war? It's a question without an answer. Very probably he didn't know himself. Much has been written in recent years arguing that the West misread the Soviet threat in postwar Europe, that in fact Stalin's ambitions were limited to the territories over which he did establish control.

Arguments about an absolute dictator's ambitions are interesting, but they are not necessarily instructive. What is instructive for this book, I believe, were the perceptions that British and American officials had of Soviet behavior and ambitions. These perceptions were essentially honest, if not invariably wise. Politicians seldom act on the basis of wisdom; they must depend on their instincts and what they're told by people they put faith in. The attitudes toward the Soviet Union that evolved in Britain and America after the war were suspicious, and eventually hostile. Only tiny splinter groups in each country argued against this general point of view: virtually all experts, the diplomats on the spot, the statesmen (both real and self-anointed) shared a skepticism and later a fear of Stalin and his intentions.

It was easy for politicians in London and Washington to accept this conventional wisdom, and it would have been nearly impossible for them to reject it. It conformed with what was known of Stalin: that he was a cruel and absolute leader who had killed tens of thousands of his countrymen in the purges of the 1930s°; who had made a cynical deal with Hitler and quickly devoured the territory Hitler had offered him; and who then ignored all the signs and warnings of an impending Nazi attack, leaving the Russian

---

° Tens of thousands was a credible estimate for the number of Stalin's victims after the war; information made available since then, by Nikita S. Khrushchev and others, suggests that an accurate figure is between five and ten million.

armies and countryside vulnerable to terrible devastation in the first months of the war. He promoted a cult of his own personality that compared with Hitler's, and conducted a propaganda campaign after the war which repeatedly emphasized the inevitability of future conflict between communism and capitalism. This was not the sort of record that inspired Western confidence.

The hostile view of the Soviet Union which made possible the Truman Doctrine also conformed to the apparent course of events after the war. One of the objects of this book is to demonstrate how the developments of 1945–47 persuaded American and British politicians and officials that they could control Soviet power only by exercising their own. Hindsight makes possible the luxury of speculation on the narrow vision and insufficient respect for Soviet concerns that may have prevailed in London and Washington after the war. But the important fact for this book is that it didn't look that way at the time.

Nor does the perspective of hindsight or any new evidence prove that Stalin could have been appeased in 1946 and 1947. To argue that appeasement was impossible is stubborn and unrealistic; historical impossibilities can never be proved. But to argue that Stalin could have been satisfied without much difficulty defies both common sense and the available evidence.

One historical tidbit that has been widely ignored deserves mention here: an interview given by Maxim Litvinov, the Soviet Commissar for Foreign Affairs before the war and an assistant foreign minister in June 1946, when he met with Richard C. Hottelet of the Columbia Broadcasting System.

Hottelet asked Litvinov how he saw the prospects for East-West cooperation. "The outlook is bad," Litvinov replied. "It seems as though the differences between East and West have gone too far to be reconciled. . . ." Why? Litvinov cited two reasons. First: "There has been a return in Russia to the outmoded concept of security in terms of territory—the more you've got, the safer

12

you are." And second: "As far as I'm concerned, the root cause is the ideological conception prevailing here [Moscow] that conflict between the Communist and capitalist worlds is inevitable."

Hottelet asked what the result would be if the Western powers acquiesced to then-current Soviet demands regarding Trieste, the Italian colonies, the Danube "and the rest." Litvinov replied, "It would lead to the West being faced, after a more-or-less short time, with the next series of demands."

When Litvinov gave this interview* he was in disfavor, and he was no admirer of Stalin's diplomacy. Perhaps his testimony is tainted. On the other hand, he was in a better position to judge this question than many of the Western experts who have presumed to judge it since. Litvinov's observations are a reminder that there was good reason in 1946 to suspect Stalin's intentions.

The uncertainty about Stalin's ambitions is a good example of the inherent disorderliness of politics. Personalities and events seldom fit neatly together; instead they join in temporary combinations, then fall back into confusion. This book reflects that fact with a certain disorderliness of its own. I have made an arbitrary decision to describe domestic and foreign politics separately, on the theory that the relationship between the two is seldom precise, though always significant. Domestic politics does not so much control diplomacy as it creates the political environment in which diplomacy is conducted.

Though British and American politics both moved toward the denouement of the Truman Doctrine during 1946–47, they moved along entirely different paths. Their conjunction in March 1947,

* Hottelet did not use the interview at the time, fearing that Stalin would not forgive Litvinov, who was already in disgrace, for such indiscretion. Hottelet did tell the U.S. embassy in Moscow about his talk, and the embassy cabled its contents to Washington at once. Ambassador Walter Bedell Smith noted at the end of his cable, "Extent of this statement . . . is simply amazing to us." Hottelet finally published the interview in January 1952, after Litvinov's death.

was largely coincidental. I could find no neat way to overcome this asymmetry, so it appears (perhaps confusingly) in the book.

Throughout, I have sought to describe accurately what really happened. What might have been is another subject altogether.

—R.G.K.

Moscow, August 1973

CHAPTER I

"In those things which will increasingly
count, we can claim to lead the world."
—Herbert Morrison, *Leader of the
House of Commons, September 28,
1946.*

Herbert Morrison's optimism about Britain's place in the world, expressed at a meeting of the Labour party's regional council in Manchester, must have sounded odd to those listening. What did count? In the fall of 1946 the British public must have felt that such things as meat, eggs and a place to live counted most of all. And Britain did not lead the world in providing those commodities; it did not even lead Europe, or northern Europe. At the end of that rainy summer, the British Isles were not a congenial place to be.

Peace seemed little better than war. Wartime rationing and restrictions had actually been tightened. Millions of men had returned home and begun work, but somehow the fruits of their labor were not visible. British manufacturers advertised their products in newspapers and magazines not to promote sales (they had little or nothing to sell), but simply to remind the public of brand names. "Jaguar cars will be back soon," they promised.

Only young children who had no memory of prewar "luxury" were immune to the sense of deprivation which plagued everyone else. Anyone who remembered cigarettes, full-strength beer, whisky, large pieces of chocolate, new clothes or a new car remembered them wistfully. The papers carried pictures of British-made consumer goods coming off production lines, but the captions invariably included some version of the most irritating cliché of those days: "These goods are not yet available for the home market; they are for export."

Because Britain had "won" the war, the British people were convinced that they deserved a better future. Partly because they remembered the disappointments of the postwar twenties (when wartime promises of a "home for heroes" were inexplicably forgotten), and largely because they recalled so vividly the deprivations of the thirties, the British people had elected a Labour government on July 5, 1945, to give them a better deal. More than a year later, that Labour government had not broken any promises, and it had kept a great many, but life was hardly any better. It was sadly typical that the government's most popular innovation, the National Health Service, which Parliament had enacted on July 26, 1946, would not begin to operate for two years. At least there was no mood of national despair. There had to be *some* spoils for the victors.

Waiting for those spoils to materialize was uncomfortable. Not only luxuries were rare—there was never even enough meat. In 1946 and 1947, the average ration of meat was about a pound a week for an adult man—that is, not quite two and a quarter ounces a day, or about two good mouthfuls. Fresh eggs were seldom available; oranges and milk were similarly rare. Bacon, sugar, butter and lard were parsimoniously allocated, and virtually every other commodity had a value in "points." An average housewife had a quota of about twenty points a month. Only starchy foods were plentiful. Potatoes were never rationed, though in February 1947, the amount of potatoes available was cut by 20 percent. Nor was bread ever scarce, even after rationing began in July 1946, although it could taste awful and look alarmingly gray.

The government controlled the cost of living, though at great expense. It was official policy to maintain the cost of living at 32 percent above the 1938 level; in 1946, this cost the Exchequer more than £300 million (with the pound sterling then worth $4.00, this was more than $1.2 billion). But it worked. On a government scale which established September 1939 price levels as 100, the working class's cost of living was 129 in September 1942, and 131 in September 1946. Among major nations only Canada was less affected by wartime inflation. During this period, British workers' wages rose substantially. Industrial earnings averaged 75/10d. ($15.20) in July 1942, and 101/– ($20.20) in October 1946. Still, this was hardly an affluent wage. Even if it had been, there was little to buy.

At least jobs were plentiful. Almost everyone could find work, including the men and women being demobilized ("demobbed") at a furious rate during late 1945 and 1946. From the end of the war until the end of August 1946, nearly four million men and women reentered civilian life from the armed forces. (By March 1947, another half million soldiers were home.) But if they had little trouble finding work, housing was quite another matter. These millions of servicemen, plus 160,000 Poles who remained in Britain after the war, often had no homes to go to. At the end of the summer in 1946, many of them were so exasperated with the lack of living accommodation that they took action that was—by British standards—surprisingly rash. They moved into homes which were not their own.

The first "squatters" were discovered that summer in deserted army and R.A.F. camps. The simple huts on these bases were hardly plush, but they were rainproof. In August 20,000 people were said to have taken up such lodgings. In September the British Communist party brought squatting to the city, with substantial popular support. The first wave of several hundred families who occupied a vacant apartment building in the wealthy London district of Kensington were soon followed by thousands more. For several weeks, squatters commandeered living space in expensive London houses and flats. Because legitimate owners and the police could control water, gas and electricity, the squatter's life was never comfortable, and few took long-term possession. But the squatters made their point, and the government promised action.

It was a bleak autumn, and there were few signs that life would soon improve. Because the summer had been especially rainy, the harvest was only mediocre. Optimistic rumors that bread rationing might soon end circulated in late September and early October, but were firmly denied by the Minister of Food, John Strachey, in Parliament on October 8. Also in October, weather forecasters began predicting an unusually cold winter. As early as September 21, an official of the National Union of Mineworkers warned that if coal production was not improved, "the nation is headed for bankruptcy." In November Strachey had more sad news; the distillation of whisky, forbidden since the previous spring because of the shortage of cereals, could not begin again in the foreseeable future.

A feeling that had first grown up during the war seemed to linger: that one's life was effectively controlled by other people, and now they were making a mess of it. Optimists and pessimists both seemed foolish, and the future was completely uncertain. The material goods everyone talked about were available only on the expensive black market—the haunt of the "spiv." He was a new character in British life, one of the few scoundrels whom the English people have ever treated indulgently. A spiv could provide a temporary link with what used to be (and, said the optimists, what would come again)—a pair of stockings, a tiny bottle of perfume, some wool for a sweater. The spiv had what everybody wanted—at a price, often a ridiculous one.

Christmas was not much of a holiday in 1946. No one was hungry, but millions of people were cramped and cold. If there was a tree in the drawing room, there was not much to put under it. More likely, Aunt Mary and Uncle George were in the drawing room, waiting for a flat to become available.

Snow fell in many areas of the country on January 6th, and again on the 7th. A Ministry of Fuel official in Leeds said, "We do not wish to create alarm, but the present situation in regard to coal is very difficult." However, the temperature rose, the snow disappeared on the 8th, and such warnings were forgotten. The weather turned almost balmy—55 degrees in London on January 16th. The thaw ended a week later, and on Saturday the 25th, most of Britain awoke to find snow falling. It snowed and blew most of the weekend. By Monday morning, the entire country was under a white blanket up to four inches thick, and transport was delayed in many areas. The snow continued Monday and Tuesday. At 3 A.M. Tuesday, the temperature in London was 15 degrees, the coldest recorded since 1940.

That was how the fierce and bitter winter of 1947 began. Before it ended, it was very much worse—the worst winter of the century, by unanimous acclamation. In the first two weeks of bad weather, many generating stations had to cut electricity output, some by 25 percent, and gas pressure was dangerously low. Villagers were marooned by snowdrifts; German prisoners of war helped to clear the roads. The Society for the Prevention of Cruelty to Animals asked that table scraps be left outside for the birds, and that pets be allowed to sleep inside. Many factories closed, some because it was too cold to work, others because coal and electricity were scarce. If management did not close down, workers often walked out, protesting that the hands refused to work in such temperatures. When they got home, they often found the water pipes frozen.

There had been warnings of a possible coal shortage—like the Leeds bureaucrat's mentioned earlier—but aggravated by this incredible weather, shortage became famine. On February 5, the Ministry of Fuel and Power announced that "a most serious situation has arisen." Two days later, the Minister of Fuel, blustering, intelligent, but egocentric Emanuel Shinwell, gave his astounded colleagues in the Cabinet some very bad news: coal had virtually run out and, because of the weather, it could neither be dug nor transported fast enough to avert a disaster. As a result, he wanted to cut electricity supplies drastically (most electricity was produced by coal-fired generators) to industrial and domestic consumers in most parts of Britain. Shinwell addressed the Cabinet on Friday morning, and he announced the cuts to Parliament that same afternoon. It was "Black Friday," the beginning of the "fuel crisis."

While the country shivered and industry came to a halt, an army of men dug and shipped coal as fast as they could. Sunday work was common in the mines and on the barges and trains which brought coal from the mining areas of the north to the industrial Midlands and the south. There was no lack of cooperation from the workers. On March 3, the government decided that enough coal had been accumulated to turn the lights back on. But by then, the world had seen how vulnerable the country was. Quite suddenly, Great Britain appeared dangerously frail.*

The fuel crisis brought the Labour government to the nadir of its popularity. Although there had been reports earlier in the winter that coal might run short, government ministers had also made numerous optimistic predictions. Unfortunately, one of the most optimistic had come from Mr. Shinwell himself: "I want to tell you that there is not going to be a crisis in coal—if by crisis you mean that industrial organization is going to be seriously dislocated and that hundreds of factories are going to be closed down," he said in October. The public was not pleased to reread that perverse prophecy in February, when most newspapers reprinted it. Not only was the public mightily disturbed by the crisis; Sir Hartley Shawcross, the Government's Attorney General, added a dash of official gloom in a speech on February 8: "Certainly," he said, "if we don't succeed in overcoming this situation and improving coal production, the Labour government will fail, and there will be an end to any idea of socialism in our time." That last sonorous phrase has since taken its place in the lore of the Labour party, though the shivering nation paid scant attention to the speech at the time.

---

* The implications of the fuel crisis for Britain's foreign policy will be considered in Chapter VI.

"Socialism in our time" had become a distinct possibility in July 1945, when the British people surprised the whole world, and even themselves, by electing the Labour party to power with a large parliamentary majority. Only the Gallup Poll, accorded no great respect at the time, had predicted a Labour victory. Less scientific but more eloquent observers agreed almost unanimously that Winston Churchill could not be defeated. Most of the electorate voted on July 5, but to allow for full participation of soldiers still overseas, the ballots were not counted until July 26. When they were, a startled world learned that Labour had gained 227 seats for a new total of 393; the Conservatives and their allies lost 203, and were left with only 213. It was a rout.

During the campaign Churchill and some of his supporters predicted that a Labour government would institute a new gestapo in Britain, but no such disaster occurred. The Labour party was not a body of militant red-shirts in 1946, but an established political party supported by much of the middle class. Five members of Attlee's first Cabinet had served under Churchill in the War Cabinet, all of them prominent figures in the Labour party. This was undoubtedly an important electoral advantage. The public did not doubt Labour's ability to govern. The party was determined to inaugurate a "revolution," though it could be said that its program only compensated for a hiatus in evolution during the 1920s and 1930s. Labour's vision was not new in 1946; it had been developing for more than twenty years. And Labour's Prime Minister, Clement Attlee, a strictly middle-class little man with a bushy moustache, could not bear comparison with Marx or Lenin. He was much too modest in outlook and ambition—much too *English*.

During his first active and extremely successful year in office, Attlee made only one change in his Cabinet. It remained, in August 1946, a collection of elderly (their average age was more than 60), dedicated politicians, many of whom had very little in common save loyalty to the Labour party. The best of them were excellent ministers, and the worst were not as bad as many had

21

expected of a party which had not held office for fifteen years. Ernest Bevin, once the powerful general secretary of the immense Transport and General Workers Union who served under Churchill during the war, was Foreign Secretary, though he had wanted to be Chancellor of the Exchequer.

The Chancellor was Hugh Dalton, educated at Eton and a lecturer at the London School of Economics, who had hoped to be Foreign Secretary. Sir Stafford Cripps, once a leader of Labour's extreme left wing and Britain's ambassador to Russia early in the war, was President of the Board of Trade. The leader of the House of Commons and Lord President of the Council was Herbert Morrison, who also had general responsibility for economic planning. He was a man of humble origins and strong opinions, who had been a member of the second Labour government in 1930–31, and of the War Cabinet. The most serious challenges to Attlee's leadership were made on Morrison's behalf, and with his connivance.

Of these five men, only Attlee and Bevin were friendly enough to relax with one another. Otherwise, the Cabinet seemed more a setting for intrigue than efficient cooperation. Dalton and Bevin did not get along well, perhaps because Dalton felt himself in competition with Bevin. He wanted very much to be foreign secretary, and must have resented Attlee's last-minute decision to give the job to Bevin. Bevin distrusted and disliked Morrison for his lack of loyalty to Attlee. Morrison had small regard for Dalton—he wrote years later that as Chancellor of the Exchequer (a job Dalton had to relinquish in the fall of 1947, after disclosing the contents of his budget speech to a newspaper reporter just before delivering it), he "had little flair for administration" and was not informed about facts important to his work.

There were other strong personalities in the government, and other animosities. Two ministers who played important roles were Shinwell, the Minister of Fuel, and Aneurin Bevan, a crusading left-winger who had followed Cripps out of the Labour party in 1939 to demonstrate his support for a popular front with the

Communists. Bevan was Minister of Health and architect of the National Health Service. Shinwell was widely and heartily disliked inside the government. Dalton thought him "an awkward colleague, always thinking about himself, tensely self-centered but uncooperative [sic] with colleagues, and terribly long-winded in Cabinet and in committee, with a big chip on his shoulder always visible." According to Dalton, Bevin agreed. He quotes the foreign secretary's comment on the observation that Shinwell was his own worst enemy: "Not while I'm alive," Bevin was supposed to have said. Bevan had no love for Bevin, a confusing situation for foreigners, who often thought they were the same man. Bevan once quoted "someone" saying about Bevin, "He's a big bumblebee caught in a web, and he thinks he's the spider."

These differences inside the Cabinet were well hidden in the first year of Labour government when things seemed to go smoothly. But during the summer of 1946, when Labour's honeymoon ended so abruptly with the introduction of bread rationing,* the jealousies began to appear, and perhaps they interfered with the smooth operation of the government. In any event, Attlee's Cabinet was something else than the leadership of a religious crusade.

In the fall and winter of 1946, the Labour government did not enjoy strong popular support. Polls conducted in August and October showed about as many people dissatisfied with the government's record as were satisfied with it. (Attlee personally was better liked; throughout the fall more than 50 percent of the electorate approved his handling of his job.) Parliament had already approved the most glamorous of Labour's election promises—especially the National Health Service. The King's speech on November 12 promised nationalization of land transport and electricity, a health service for Scotland, a commission to

---

* The decision to begin bread rationing was perhaps the most difficult taken by Attlee's cabinet in its first year, and it caused confusion and frustration inside the government. Strachey proposed it, Dalton recorded in his diary, but had last-minute doubts. Other doubters forced a last-minute review of the question after an ostensibly final decision to ration bread had been reached.

COLD WINTER, COLD WAR

buy and sell raw cotton, a law to improve the organization of "a number of important industries," and several other minor measures. The speech revealed the Attlee government's gravest weakness—its preoccupation with past grievances, and relative disregard for the future. Having disposed of the bulk of its program in the first year, it had no new ideas. None of the rather dreary proposals of that 1946 King's speech caught the imagination of a weary electorate that was conscious above all of the hundreds of comforts, big and small, still denied it.

The government's prestige suffered a serious blow soon after the King's speech, when fifty-seven left-wing back-benchers signed a motion criticizing Bevin's foreign policy. The motion asked the government to alter its attitude and encourage collaboration with "all nations and groups striving to secure full socialist planning and control of the world's resources" to prevent a conflict between the Soviet Union and the United States. The motion came to a vote in the House after a bitter fight within the party. One hundred back-benchers abstained, although none voted against the government. The impression was clear. Labour in power was no more unified than it had been in opposition before the war, when Cripps, Bevan and others on the left wing had been expelled or resigned from the party. Not only had Attlee and his colleagues lost some of their zeal and their popularity; they also had trouble simply controlling their Labour colleagues in Parliament.

Attlee never appeared shaken by the back-benchers' revolt, or by unfavorable opinion polls, though both affected the morale of some ministers. Regardless of public opinion, the government had a great deal to do. December and January were busy months, more than filled with crises in Palestine and India, the end of negotiations for peace treaties with Germany's former satellites, talks with France for a new treaty of alliance, and an argument with Russia about whether Britain wanted to renew the Anglo-Soviet treaty—all problems which Britain could not ignore.

At home the Cabinet undertook a long review of foreign and

domestic policy in early January. To welcome the new year, London's truck drivers went on strike, and troops had to be used to deliver meat and other essential goods. Then the fuel crisis. And these were only the events which were recorded in the newspapers; no doubt, the government had other problems.

The fuel crisis seems to have brought out the worst in many Cabinet members. Shinwell has recalled that there was a "terrible cold war going on inside the Cabinet" at the time. The Minister of Fuel and Power was himself the subject of much bitterness; many of his colleagues held Shinwell personally responsible for the crisis. While the country froze, the government appeared to be adrift—"our public relations weren't very good," in the words of one minister. During the weekend after "Black Friday," rumors flew (mostly to and from Conservative newspapers, but elsewhere too) about the possibility of Labour opting for a coalition government to get out of the crisis. (Shinwell spent the weekend alone in his ministry, working without even the encouragement of a telephone call from Attlee.)

The crisis evoked little sympathy from the public. In March the Gallup Poll found 54 percent of the people dissatisfied with their government; only 39 percent were satisfied.* Attlee's personal popularity also suffered. Only 46 percent approved of his performance, and 45 percent disapproved. "This had not been the end of the world, as some panic-mongers had expected," Dalton wrote later, "but it was certainly the first really heavy blow to confidence in the Government and in our postwar plans. This soon began to show itself in many different and unwelcome ways. Never glad, confident morning again."

The fuel crisis had another important effect. It was a pointed reminder that Britain's worst problems were economic ones, and that some economic problems are absolutely fundamental.

---

* The figures in December had been 43 percent satisfied, 42 percent dissatisfied, and 15 percent without an opinion. But in the March 1947, survey, only seven percent had no opinion. Perhaps the fuel crisis made up a lot of minds.

It was a widely accepted "fact" after the war that Britain was a temporarily impoverished Great Power, but a Great Power nevertheless. The implication of this view was that the war had left Britain financially exhausted, but still potentially very strong, and still capable of exerting enormous influence. British politicians generally agreed that Russia and America would become the world's most important nations, more powerful than any the world had yet known. But in 1945 and 1946, there was no doubt either that Britain would continue to have immense power and importance in world affairs. That assumption was popular and not easily dispelled, but the fuel crisis dispelled it, at least for the world outside Britain. (Polls showed that the British people still regarded their country as a great power. In March 1947, three-fourths of them thought Britain would be one of the world's three major powers in 1972.)

The fundamental fact—as yet undiscovered—was that the war had left Britain without the resources necessary to maintain its former world position. The political leaders of the time saw it slightly differently. They apparently thought that Britain required immense financial aid, but if it was secured, a good recovery from the war was possible. So in 1944, John Maynard Keynes had negotiated a loan of $3.75 billion in Washington, and an additional $1.25 billion from Canada. These huge credits were expected to bring Britain through the difficulties of readjusting to peacetime. Official estimates as late as January 1947 predicted that these borrowed North American dollars would last until early 1949. But even this rate of depletion was faster than originally hoped, both because Britain needed more goods from the dollar area than had been anticipated, and because the prices of American goods went up rapidly because of post-war inflation. Dalton wrote in his diary that the dollar's value, measured in terms of American wholesale prices, fell 30 percent between the time the U.S. loan was negotiated in December 1945 and the spring of 1947. (The dollar credits were virtually wiped out in a financial crisis of mid-1947, which followed the fuel crisis.)

According to Attlee, economists had warned the wartime coalition government that the failure to maintain normal patterns of industrial investment during the war would eventually cause serious economic difficulties. But the government seemed to think that whatever problems developed would be financial, and neither as fundamental nor as significant as they eventually proved to be. (Attlee has also said that the weather of 1947 was more responsible for the subsequent economic crisis than any other factor.) But even an uncanny official awareness of Britain's problems would hardly have been much help, because the necessary remedies were beyond the government's capabilities. They all involved money, and almost no money was available.

In late 1946 every important sector of the economy was in trouble. Exports, the most important sector of all, were inadequate and not improving. The total value of British exports in July 1946 was £89 million ($356 million), in August £78 million, in September £74 million, then slowly back up, reaching £90 million in December. The average visible monthly trade deficit in 1946 was about £28 million (almost $112 million), and it improved only marginally in the first months of 1947. Imports continued at a high level, and most of them were bought in the dollar area.

The balance of payments deficit for 1946 was £348 million ($1.392 billion), of which £332 million, or more than 95 percent, was incurred in trade with dollar-area nations. Yet this deficit was grounds for some optimism in the fall. Keynes and his advisors in Washington had assumed the year before that the 1946 deficit would be about £750 million. When it turned out to be less than half that, some officials took it as a good sign.

Others, like Sir Stafford Cripps, were more cautious, and correctly so. The deficit was lower than expected because Britain could not buy all the imports it wanted—they were not available on the world market. In fact, the economy would have been in better condition if the 1946 deficit had been £750 million—that would have meant that vital machinery and raw materials had been bought and were in use. As it was, worn-out machinery was not being replaced, and raw materials were in painfully short supply. Industrial production was stagnant. The statistics for the production of coal, the country's most important commodity, were perhaps most revealing of all: in 1940, Britain produced 224.3 million tons; in 1946, only 190.06 million. Yet the country's needs were greater than in 1940.

The government prepared a good summary of the economy's problems in February 1947, published as a white paper on February 21. According to it, "The central fact of 1947 is that we have not enough resources to do all that we want to do. We have barely enough to do all that we must do." It was a glum analysis, but accompanying statistics confirmed its accuracy. At the end of 1946, brick production was half the 1938 level, cotton was 40 percent below 1938, wool 20 percent. Food production in all areas but livestock was slightly better than 1938, but consumption was higher too. Not until the third quarter of 1946 did exports by volume equal 1938, and they were still not worth as much. But this could not have been too surprising. When the war ended, only 2 percent of Britain's manpower was engaged in producing exports.

The February white paper came too late to surprise anyone with its statistics. Its implications became visible to the ordinary man's eye as 1947 (*Annus horrendus,* Dalton once called it) began. Brick and cotton producers both announced early in January that a shortage of coal would force them to cut production. Train services were reduced to conserve coal, and in mid-January Sir Stafford Cripps announced that industry generally would have its coal allocation cut by 50 to 60 percent for six weeks, though there would be extra coal for vital industries, and electricity production would proceed "full out."

His announcement would have been more serious if the previous allocations had ever been met. In fact, Sir Stafford was telling the industrial community that instead of promising it about twice as much coal as was ever delivered, he was balancing promises and supplies more realistically. Even the *Daily Express,* Labour's most emotional critic, blamed someone besides the government for the coal shortage. "The coal crisis began in 1940," said the *Express*, "when the youngest and strongest miners were allowed to leave the pits to join the army or go back into other industries. They have never come back." Manpower shortages in the mines remained a serious problem after the war. The gap between production and consumption of coal in January 1947 was 300,000 tons a week. As a result, the four-day week was common in many industries well before the fuel crisis began officially on February 7. Obviously, the weather was not entirely to blame. It seems likely that there would have been serious coal shortages even if January and February had been normal winter months, and coal consumption was undoubtedly lower than normal during the two weeks of warm weather in mid-January, a fact which must have reduced the impact of the crisis when it came a fortnight later.

The dramatic effects of the fuel crisis itself, in which more than 2.3 million men were temporarily put out of work, obviously exaggerated Britain's problems, but these exaggerations were instructive. The *Observer* seemed to catch one implication of Black Friday with painful accuracy in an editorial on February 16: "How do Mr. Attlee's apparently so sensible exhortations for an all-out production drive sound now, when we can see that industry was in fact being driven on waning fuel reserves to a complete standstill?"

That question or one like it would have been asked sometime during 1947 even without a fuel crisis. As Attlee himself has recalled, there was a holiday from industrial investment during the war which deprived Britain of invaluable new plants and equipment. Much of the economic infrastructure was worn out—a disability which remained important for many years after 1947. Yet Britain's economic health depended (as it still does) on the country's ability to produce many more goods than it consumed, and at low enough costs to make the goods competitive in the world market. Old factories and tired machinery (not to mention the shortages of raw materials which, except for coal, could not be

29

controlled) did not lend themselves to such production, even
when encouraged by the most inspiring exhortations that politicians could contrive.

And exhort they did. Attlee, Morrison, Cripps, Dalton and all
the others spoke time and again about the need to produce, to
work harder, to keep shoulders down and chins up. But they did
little else. The American and Canadian loans were of great assistance, and were important political achievements, but they were
desperate requirements, not aspects of a coherent economic
policy.

When lend-lease abruptly ended, Britain was in danger of
bankruptcy. Money had to be found somewhere; it was found in
North America. (Even then, some members of the Cabinet,
including Bevan and Shinwell, opposed the loan. They thought it
was unnecessary, and tied Britain too closely to the United States.)
The Labour party had loudly promised economic planning in
1945, but planning was more a slogan than a reality. The leaders of
the party reached political maturity in an era when jobs were
scarce and the worker's lot a poor one. They were ill-equipped for
a time when the shortage was not of jobs, but of goods for com-
panies to sell and workers to buy. (In fairness, all of Britain's
politicians were unprepared for the course the economy took after
the war.)

Old socialist principles had no apparent application to the
problems of 1946–47, but the government came up with no up-
to-date substitutes. The only really original idea for coping with
shortages was the remarkable groundnut (peanut) scheme, and it
turned out to be utterly impractical.

The plan was announced in a white paper on February 5, 1947,
after several months of prior investigation, and it appeared to be
of unassailable intelligence and great compassion. The groundnut
scheme would end Britain's chronic shortage of fats and oils, and
bring prosperity and progress to much of British East Africa.
Under the careful supervision of 749 European experts, 32,100
Africans would grow peanuts on 3,250,000 acres of specially

selected ground in areas scattered through Tanganyka, Northern Rhodesia and Kenya. Profits would improve the life of the Africans, and peanuts would improve the diet of the British. "Credit should be given to the enlightened men who have worked out this stimulating departure in policy, which is so large in promise," said *The Times*.

Promise was never fulfilled. The planners of the groundnut scheme did not know as much as they should have about the problems of growing peanuts in East Africa. Neither the soil nor the climate was quite right. The first crops did badly, some of them failing completely. The project soon stumbled to a quiet death. The millions of pounds it cost disappeared into the East African terrain leaving hardly a trace.

Peanuts did not distract the public or members of the government for very long. The general impression remained that men had woefully little control over events. Inside the Cabinet, recriminations seemed more popular than new ideas. Morrison, who clearly had failed to produce the kind of planning his colleagues had hoped for and expected, was able to write of Dalton later that "he was unaware of the financial crisis of 1947 until he was in the midst of it." Shinwell accepted no blame at all, and thought the fuel crisis wasn't a fuel crisis at all—"it was a transport crisis," he has said, and with some justification. (What coal there was could not be moved to the places where it was needed because of weather conditions during the crisis.)

Some ministers seemed eager to find scapegoats. Dalton, Morrison, Cripps and George Isaacs, the Minister of Labor, found one while working together as the Ministerial Committee on Economic planning. They recommended to the Cabinet in January that drastic moves be taken to provide more men to work in industry. Their principal suggestion was to increase the rate of demobilization substantially, and it was overwhelmingly rejected by the Cabinet on the grounds that the national defense had to take priority. In an angry message to Attlee afterward, Dalton threatened to resign "if my views on such important matters were to continue to be brushed aside as of no account." He warned Attlee of the pressing danger "of economic and financial over-strain and collapse."

This incident seems to have been typical of the way the Cabinet made its decisions in those months. Resources were scarce and every minister had plans for using some of them. Shinwell recalled years later, "The scarcer the resources, the fiercer the competition among ministers." This was not planning, and it did not encourage the kind of cooperative effort planning required. On the contrary, such "supply and demand" government encouraged animosities inside the Cabinet, and eventually left Attlee and his colleagues holding a distinctly empty bag, without any good explanations for where the contents had gone. ("At some point we ought to have told the country the truth," Shinwell said years afterward.)

Throughout this period, the government had one obvious option that would reduce state spending—cutting overseas expenditures. Only Bevin, the foreign secretary, spoke in defense of these funds, and even his enthusiasm was limited. Dalton told the House of Commons on March 6, 1947, that in the two previous years, Britain had spent £87 million ($348 million) aiding Greece and £82 million ($328 million) supporting Palestine. In 1946, food for the British zone of Germany cost the Treasury £80 million ($320 million). These seemed the three most superfluous items in the overseas budget, and together they amounted to more than £140 ($640) million a year. There were many other overseas costs which must have appealed to ministers in search of expendables—in India, Egypt and elsewhere. By the winter of 1947 it was difficult to argue with those who asked that these commitments be reduced or eliminated. What business had a country in Britain's condition trying to maintain them?

CHAPTER II

"Had Enough?"
—The Republican Party's
slogan in the American
congressional election
of 1946.

The discomforts of war are best endured by exaggerating the comforts of peace. The worse the war, the better the peace must certainly be. In the general election of 1945, the British people had an opportunity to try to make that illusion a reality, and they elected a Labour government. The American people had no occasion to "begin again" after World War II. Peace brought no new government. Despite America's anxious hopes, a better world did not appear.

"That wonderful figure, the buoyant, happy American who knew all the answers or blithely assumed they would turn up, has finally come up against the realities of the scientific age he did so much to create," wrote James Reston early in August 1946, almost a year after the war had ended. "Like a strong and carefree young man who is suddenly called upon to assume the responsibilities of maturity, he is slightly dazed and may even be a little resentful. If this is what is meant by 'coming of age,' he isn't sure he likes it, though he candidly admits that he can scarcely escape it. . . ."

Life was difficult and annoying that August, and it was improving only slowly. Many problems distracted the mind and added to one's bewilderment, but three stood out, the most disrupting and frustrating of all: too many consumer goods were in short supply, prices were too high and rising, and there were too many strikes. None of them was even vaguely as serious as Britain's problems, and by British standards, the discomforts they caused were marginal indeed. But the comparison is not fair; the British could see *why* life was hard—the effects of war were obvious. Americans saw no good reasons why wartime conditions had to persist so long after the war was over. But with reason or without, many of the war's discomforts endured and persisted.

The shortages were especially perplexing. During the war, people understood why a good steak was so hard to find, or a new car not available. By August 1946, that kind of patience was exhausted. People wanted houses, and despite the fact that hundreds of thousands were being built, those who could not find one felt cheated or worse. Those who had a house wanted furniture for it, or clothes for themselves. Because people saw no reason for being denied so many goods, they seemed less reluctant to seek them in irregular places. The black market thrived in late summer and fall of 1946 in a way unknown during the war, when a gallon of illicit gasoline might have been stolen from army supplies, and thus have impeded the war effort. Now there was no war effort, and no apparent reason to go without.

Some consumer goods did reappear. In early August the Reconstruction Finance Corporation released enough cloth to make one million men's suits and overcoats, and distillers were allocated enough grain to make substantial quantities of liquor. (Beer was usually available, though brewers were limited to 70 percent of their 1945 production.) Perhaps stimulated by the nearness of November's congressional elections, the Civilian Production Administration decided in late October that there was enough cloth to allow the nation's dress manufacturers to follow Paris's New Look, dropping hemlines to mid-calf or below. Several days later, bread loaves which had been reduced in size by 10 percent returned to normal.

But these improvements were hardly noticed because the country was preoccupied with a shortage of meat. In the second half of 1946, almost everyone in the United States was either short of meat or paying exorbitant prices to get enough of it. Meat was America's most popular topic of conversation; it became a symbol of all the frustrations of postwar life. For seven weeks during the summer, there were adequate supplies, but at extraordinarily high prices. Apart from that brief period, there was not enough. Many cities went entirely without meat on some days. Housewives spent hours in butchers' queues for half a dozen hot dogs or a half pound of bacon. Cheese soufflé became a popular dish; clever mothers convinced innocent children that it was a rare delicacy, ever so much better than roast beef.

Until the end of June, the price of meat had been controlled by the Office of Price Administration (O.P.A.), the government agency which controlled the prices of almost everything during and after the war. For many Americans, especially in the business community, O.P.A. had become a symbol of every uncomfortable and expendable aspect of wartime American life. The agency interfered with private lives and private initiative, and had no place in the postwar United States which they imagined. Millions of others held no such strong opinions, but nevertheless waited eagerly for the day when O.P.A. and all the war's paraphernalia would disappear. President Truman, however, thought O.P.A. could not be treated as a symbol; he regarded it as important and perhaps necessary to the success of "reconversion," as the change back to peacetime life was called. In January 1946, he asked Congress to extend the life of O.P.A., which was due to expire in June, for another year.

The resulting fight was one of the liveliest in the early days of Truman's presidency. Business and industry, led vociferously by the National Association of Manufacturers, lobbied intensely against renewing O.P.A. Trade unions, consumer groups and unorganized citizens defended it. In the end both lost. Truman vetoed the first bill Congress passed in June, which would have continued O.P.A. in theory but crippled it in practice with a series of debilitating amendments. His veto temporarily ended all price controls, creating ferocious inflation.

In August Congress passed a second extension of O.P.A.'s authority, and Truman accepted it. This bill stipulated that controls on meat prices could be reestablished on August 20, but not before, and only if it seemed absolutely necessary.

This last stipulation was disastrous. In the hope that controls would be removed, meat producers had hoarded large quantities of beef, pork and lamb. When controls did end on June 30 (and prices shot up 30 to 80 percent), this hoarded supply was dumped onto the market, where in Truman's words it was "gobbled up immediately by the meat-hungry people, and created more shortage." The demand was so great that farmers decided to slaughter many animals well before they were mature. When August 20 finally arrived, the Price Decontrol Board established by the new law decided, not surprisingly, that there was no alternative to reinstituting controls. But it was already too late to improve the situation; the mechanisms of price controls had almost disappeared during the seven weeks they had been inoperative, and the producers had insured another shortage by rushing so much meat to market prematurely.

The public was unwilling or unable to realize this, and soon, when shortages did develop again, whatever sympathy had existed for O.P.A. quickly disappeared. Truman and other members of his administration tried to explain what had happened, but no one wanted explanations. A roast for Sunday dinner would have been much more welcome. The situation worsened, the congressional elections approached, and on October 14, the president told the country by radio that meat controls would be lifted at once and permanently. Prices again went rapidly up, but meat did not flood back to the grocery stores as it had in early July. Only several months later did supply and demand come into balance.

Meat was only one commodity whose price soared that autumn; there were hundreds of others. The O.P.A. allowed increases on many items, especially durable consumer goods which the public so eagerly sought. Cars, electrical appliances of all kinds, cotton goods and beer all went up from three to fifteen percent in six weeks. The official consumer price index for urban Americans went from 145.9 in September to 153.3 in December. The retail food price index rose from 171.2 in August to 185.9 in December. For a time near the end of 1946, it looked as though price inflation might be uncontrollable.

Prices rose for goods that were scarce. Millions of Americans had a lot of money, but having enough money was not enough. American industry was not yet producing enough goods, and rising prices in late 1946 could be blamed partially on the classic problem of demand exceeding supply. But as in the meat crisis, the facts were either not apparent or too complicated to appreciate. The public wanted scapegoats for inflation, and one obvious candidate, even the economists agreed, was rising wages.* Rising wages could be blamed on the headstrong labor unions.

America's trade unions did have serious grievances in 1946, and for the first time in five years they were prepared to make them known in the bluntest way, by going on strike. Fully 116 million man-days were lost in work stoppages in 1946 (compared to 38 million in 1945). There were almost 5,000 strikes in 1946, each of them lasting an average of 24 days. Every large community in the country was affected by industrial disputes, yet most Americans felt even further removed from the powers that caused them than from the government in Washington.

Shortages, inflation, strikes—a devastating combination, producing bitterness not mitigated by understanding. But Americans do not have to understand a problem to blame someone for causing it. In the autumn of 1946, the public's anger was directed at Harry Truman.

---

* During 1946, the average industrial wage rose 15 percent, while the consumer price index for urban Americans rose 18 percent—figures that initially suggest a wage-price spiral. A longer view alters this impression. While the price index rose more than 21 percent in 1945–46, the average industrial wage actually fell slightly in those two years. Many industries were passing on the cost of reconversion to the consumer, and this was an important contributor to the rise in prices after the war. (Statistics based on figures in the official *Statistical Abstract of the United States* for 1947 and 1948.)

Few men have come to the presidency less prepared or less eager to meet its rigorous requirements than Harry Truman, the honest haberdasher from Independence, Missouri. When Franklin D. Roosevelt died on April 12, 1945, Truman was in the capitol, presiding over the Senate and writing a letter to his mother and sister in which he hoped "that you are having a nice spell of weather." He enjoyed being vice president, a job he had held—and pursued in a relaxed manner—for only three months. Roosevelt had not brought Truman into his confidence; the vice president knew little about some of the most important affairs of state. He entered the presidency with few preconceptions about what he would like to do with it, but he was a serious student of American history, and he believed strongly in the government's ability and duty to improve the lives of the people.

Truman's own politics remained a mystery to his countrymen for the first six months of his presidency. Many expected, or hoped, that he would be a meek president, and by New Deal standards a conservative one. But he suggested quite another approach to his task in September 1945, in his first important message to Congress on domestic affairs. It was a forceful reiteration of Roosevelt's "Economic Bill of Rights," an assertion of the government's obligation to legislate security and equal opportunity for all Americans. Truman made several specific proposals to Congress which, he said, would help fulfill that obligation, and he promised to ask for more in the following months. "That September the sixth speech was made to let the Hearsts and McCormicks know that they were not going to take me into their camp," Truman told a friend later. He was referring to William Randolph Hearst and Col. Robert McCormick, newspaper proprietors who were fervent opponents of the New Deal, and who had hoped that the Roosevelt era had died with Roosevelt. It had not.

Not that Truman was any Roosevelt. He was a straightforward man of modest origins who was intelligent, but had not gone to college. He had few illusions about himself or his capabilities, and he seldom said anything other than what he meant. His success in politics was due largely to three factors: he worked hard, he was completely honest, and he had often been in the right spot at the right moment. Because his Senate committee had done such a good job investigating profiteering and other irregularities in wartime purchasing and production, Truman's name was often heard in Washington in 1944. At the same time Vice President Henry Wallace's left-wing views suddenly seemed a liability to Roosevelt; he had to find a new running mate for the 1944 presidential election. Other names were mentioned, but for one reason or another—some of them quite bizarre—nobody but Truman seemed entirely safe, so Truman it was. °

His first months as president went quite smoothly—very smoothly, considering how little experience Truman brought to the job. His lack of experience was crucial only once, in the precipitous decision to end lend-lease aid to America's allies immediately after the end of the war. That error, though serious, had little effect on domestic politics. Truman's popularity was high according to public opinion polls—higher in May 1945 than even FDR's had ever been. But this did not last. The war ended, prices rose, shortages continued and the voters became restless.

It was unfair to blame Truman for most of what went wrong. He warned Congress that if price controls, especially for meat, were removed too quickly, the result might be disastrous. His warning was not heeded, and Congress approved the calamitous holiday on meat controls during July and August 1946. He also tried to fight inflation by controlling government spending. Early in August, he announced that government departments would have to spend $2.2 billion less in the coming year than had been expected.

But the causes of the postwar inflation were too numerous for it to be controlled by a reduction in the federal budget. Because they had saved so much during the war, Americans had money to

---

° Historians have been unable to establish exactly how or precisely why Truman was chosen as Roosevelt's running mate, although several "first-hand" versions of FDR's decision have already been recorded. Robert Sherwood, in *Roosevelt and Hopkins*, wrote that Harry Hopkins thought Roosevelt had picked Truman some time before anyone else knew it, but all the other evidence suggests it was a last-minute decision.

buy many more goods than were available or could be produced. Truman's attempt to curtail government consumption could make only a marginal difference. Any really stringent measures to reduce the purchasing power of ordinary consumers to meaningfully affect inflation would have been politically suicidal.

Truman's efforts to cope with postwar dislocations were often disguised from public view by the president's unintentional diversionary tactics. On several important occasions in 1946, Truman allowed himself to look weak. He lost that intangible advantage known as the political initiative. In the process, millions of Americans decided that their new president was a sad and pitiable bungler.

The president's first important political error was his inconsistent reaction to two national labor disputes in the spring of 1946. The first was a coal strike which lasted for forty days in April and May. While coal stocks dwindled for almost five weeks, forcing some cities to revive wartime "dim-outs," the government did nothing to stop the strike. In the fifth week, Truman ordered that the mines be seized, and the government (the new proprietors) then quickly negotiated a settlement with the miners.

There had been strong public pressure to act sooner, but Truman hesitated, apparently because he wanted to avoid any arbitrary action which might have set a precedent for punitive antilabor legislation.

Truman might have survived this incident unscathed had not two railway unions threatened to call a national railroad strike at the same time as the coal dispute. His attitude to the railwaymen belied the studied calm of his approach to the coal miners. The president lost his temper with the railroad unions, and asked Congress to give him the power to draft workers into national service to prevent a strike if the nation's interests were in jeopardy. The two unions signed a contract.

Why didn't Truman act as quickly in the coal strike? Did the president have a labor policy? The question recurred in June, when Truman vetoed a bill Congress had passed to curtail trade-union power. In fact, it was a punitive law, and Truman showed courage by rejecting it.

The president's policy on shortages was similarly unpopular, not because a better policy seemed available, but because his failed to work. The president tried to persuade the public to blame the meat crisis on Congress—and especially the Republicans in Congress—because they had withheld from him power to control meat prices, but the public blamed Truman. (Fortunately for the Republicans, they could attack the administration without offering alternative policies. When asked at the height of the meat crisis for a way to solve it, Senator Robert A. Taft, the Republicans' spokesman on domestic affairs, had curt advice: "Eat less.") When Truman himself removed controls on meat prices in October, it looked as though he had suddenly rejected what everyone thought was an article of his political faith—that price controls should not be dropped arbitrarily. Was this a strong president?

Perhaps worst of all was the "Wallace incident," Truman's clumsiest blunder as president, for which he could make no convincing excuse.

Henry Wallace, who became secretary of commerce when Truman replaced him as vice president, accepted an invitation to speak at a political rally in New York City on September 12, 1946. The party in New York was left-of-center among Democrats, and Wallace was widely regarded as the left's national leader. He decided to devote his speech to foreign policy; specifically to a plea for reasonable treatment for the Soviet Union and an attack on those who favored a "get tough with Russia" policy. The speech was described to newspapermen as "controversial" by Wallace or his aides several days before it was delivered.

Wallace came to the White House on September 10 for a general talk on the political situation with President Truman, and to show him his proposed speech. Exactly what happened at that meeting is unclear. Apparently, Wallace gave Truman a verbal outline of the speech while the president thumbed through it.* Advance copies of the speech were given to the press on the 12th, a Thursday, several hours before Truman held his weekly meeting with the press. At the news conference, the president was asked if it was true—as Wallace had written into the speech—that Truman had read and approved what the secretary of commerce was going to say in New York that night. Truman said he had.

Later, at Madison Square Garden, Wallace delivered his speech. His message was that if Britain and the United States would stop getting tough with Stalin, a meaningful peace would be possible. "The World Order is bankrupt," Wallace declared, "and the United States, Russia and England are the receivers." He called on Britain and the United States to relinquish control of their military bases around the world to the United Nations, and asked America to "study in detail just how the Russian character was formed," and to sympathize with the Soviet Union's desire for security. In sum, Wallace proposed a foreign policy that bore small resemblance to the one then being pursued by Secretary of State James Byrnes.**

The speech, with Truman's endorsement, caused an immediate and immense furor in the United States and throughout the world. Had Wallace abandoned the policy of the administration in which he served as a cabinet member? Or did this speech mean that American policy had changed? Or had Byrnes been misunderstood for several months? Byrnes's friends and allies thought bitterly that the president had cut his secretary of state adrift. Byrnes, who was trying to negotiate peace treaties in Paris at the time, was furious. The rest of the world looked on, bewildered.

* Truman has written in his memoirs that "of course there was no time for me to read the speech, even in part." However, Clark Clifford, one of Truman's closest aides, told one of the President's early biographers, Jonathan Daniels, that Truman admitted "thumbing through" the speech on September 10, two days before the speech was given.

** The significance of the Wallace incident for American foreign policy will be considered in detail in Chapter V.

For a week Truman procrastinated. A series of letters, statements and meetings only made the situation more embarrassing. Finally, eight days after Wallace's speech (and after Truman admitted that he had made a mistake), the president asked for Wallace's resignation. Eight days was a long time in the midst of a congressional election campaign. Truman's obvious blunder remained on the front page the entire time. Voters who were already confused by the behavior of the Soviet Union, and who suspected that Truman was a weak, indecisive president, felt their worst fears confirmed. A new proverb found a place in the language: "To err is Truman." Why was the president late to the meeting, wags began to ask. Well, when he woke up that morning he had been a little stiff in the joints, and it took him longer than usual to put his foot in his mouth. The Gallup Poll expressed public opinion numerically. In February 1946, 63 percent of Americans questioned approved the way President Truman handled his job. In April it was 50 percent, in July 43 percent, and in the first week of October, 32 percent.

It was left to a Boston advertising man named Karl Frost to reduce all the nation's frustration, anger and confusion to just two inquisitive words: "Had Enough?" Frost coined the slogan for local Republican candidates in Massachusetts, but it was so ideally suited to the mood of the time that it spread throughout the country like cream in coffee. "Everyone knows what they mean," wrote a *Manchester Guardian* correspondent of the Republicans' epigram, but he was falling right into their trap. The correspondent didn't say what it meant, just as the Republicans didn't, because it was a slogan designed for all men and all complaints. It was difficult to find anyone that fall who was not tempted to agree that he had had enough.

Millions of middle- and upper-class Americans thought the slogan applied to the progressivism of the New Deal—a progressivism which still angered many citizens in a country which remained impressed by the shibboleths of self-reliance and the cult of the self-made man.

One of the most popular books of 1945 was a powerful tract by a University of Chicago economist, Friedrich A. von Hayek, called *The Road to Serfdom.* (It had been published in Britain—where Hayek wrote it—in 1944.) Hayek's thesis was that nazism, socialism, and communism all grew from a common urge for economic collectivization which invariably resulted in totalitarianism. In the doubting atmosphere of postwar America, it became a best-seller. If things were going badly, perhaps it was because the legendary American businessman wasn't able to operate freely for the benefit of all; perhaps "the government" was much too involved in other people's affairs; perhaps it was time for a return to "normalcy," a Malapropish term coined by Warren Harding after World War I.

So many events of late 1946 seemed to conform to this analysis. Hadn't government meddling created shortages and inflation? Weren't the labor unions—those friends of the New Deal—behaving irresponsibly with relative immunity? Weren't the radicals like Henry Wallace causing trouble?

The appeal of such thinking was evident even before the most eager congressional candidates had begun their campaigns in early September. Many commentators were already predicting a "conservative" new Congress, and it was generally agreed that the country was "turning right." Party primaries in August seemed to confirm it. In Wisconsin, a relative unknown—a circuit judge named Joseph R. McCarthy (who did not exploit the "communism" issue at all)—defeated Senator Robert M. LaFollette Jr., one of the crusading LaFollette family which had dominated Wisconsin politics for a generation, and who had disbanded his Progressive party to run for the Republican nomination for the Senate. In New York, left-wing candidates did badly in August primaries in both parties. The Truman administration and the Democratic party, of course, were symbols of the "left" against which the country was apparently turning.

The Democrats had another problem: a meager record to run on. The session of Congress that ended in early August achieved little. The president had proposed twenty-one major pieces of legislation, and Congress had defeated thirteen, including all of the most glamorous ones. Among them were plans for national health insurance, a higher minimum wage, a fair employment practices act (requiring equal opportunities for blacks), and a universal military training act. Congress approved only six of the administration's requests, and none of them had great popular appeal. Two other proposals died in the congressional machinery. It was not much to boast about.

At the beginning of the campaign the Wallace incident bewildered and confused the Democrats. Half a dozen minor party functionaries made this clear in an interview with journalists just after they visited the president in mid-October to discuss campaign strategy. None of the politicians supported Wallace. One said his speech was "a trial balloon designed to find out the sentiment of the American people." Another said, "It's going to hurt." John W. Zimmerman, a candidate for the House of Representatives from New Jersey, had a more pointed comment: "The people think it's a screwy mess and so do I."

Truman apparently decided that he was personally more of a liability than an asset to Democratic candidates, and he made no speeches during the campaign. His one contribution was to participate in a nationwide radio program prepared by the Democratic National Committee which included the recorded voice of FDR. "A grisly stratagem," complained the Republican party chairman. But he had no reason to worry; the Republicans seemed unbeatable. A reporter's analysis of the mood of the Midwest was typical: "Basically, the voters of the Middle West seem to be 'fed up' as they have not been in years, and the balloting on November 5 promises to be the largest outpouring of angry protest votes in any off-year election since 1930...." Walter Lippmann wrote in mid-October: "We have been experiencing the transfer of power from the Democrats to the Republicans, and during this period the Democrats have reigned, but not ruled." The Gallup Poll recorded that in March, 53 percent said they would vote for Democratic congressional candidates; 47 percent chose Republicans. The Democrats slipped to 49 percent in July and 47 percent in October.

Nothing the Democrats could do would reverse the trend. Truman's last important effort was his October 14 announcement of the permanent end of meat price controls, but even this worked against him. He must have hoped that meat would flood the market as it did when price controls had been lifted in July. But the July glut had exhausted whatever surplus the producers had hoarded; the only effect of the October announcement was to send prices soaring. Angry housewives finally brought them back to more reasonable levels by boycotting butchers until prices fell. The Democratic party did not benefit from these boycotts.

On November 5, 54.3 percent of the electorate voted for Republican congressional candidates, 45.7 voted for Democrats. For the first time in almost twenty years, Republicans held a majority in the House (245–188), in the Senate (51–45) and in the nation's state capitals. In the previous Congress, Democrats had held a 57–38 advantage in the Senate (there was one independent) and a 242–190 majority in the House.

The results could hardly have been a more convincing repudiation of the Truman administration—so convincing, in fact, that when Senator J. William Fulbright suggested after the election that Truman appoint a Republican secretary of state, then resign the presidency in his favor, he was supported by Marshall Field, a relatively liberal Chicago newspaper publisher, and many others.* Truman had no such intention, but one could hardly have blamed him if he had; it was the darkest moment in his political career. When the president's train arrived at Union Station in Washington on November 6 (he had gone home to Missouri to vote), only his undersecretary of state, Dean Acheson, was there to meet him. Apparently, no other member of the official family had anything to say, or any convincing comfort to offer.

With one exception, the issues which had defeated the

---

* At that time, the secretary of state was second in the line of succession to the presidency, after the vice president. Because Truman had himself succeeded from the vice presidency, that office was vacant until after the 1948 election.

Democrats in 1946 were bread-and-butter ones. That exception was Communism. Throughout the country, and especially in the Mid- and Far West, the fear grew that communists and radicals were secretly or overtly doing their evil best to pervert American life.

The "red scare" of 1919–1920 had taught Americans the jargon of reflex anticommunism and the philosophy that all evil was un-American. Then, a war-weary country found it impossible to explain a series of labor disputes and acts of violence which, by traditional American standards, had no reasonable cause. Millions decided that Bolsheviks must have been to blame. (This view was flamboyantly defended by the attorney general of that time, A. Mitchell Palmer, who probably violated more civil rights in the pursuit of Communists in 1920 than did anyone in the heyday of Senator Joseph R. McCarthy.)

By 1946 Americans were somewhat more sophisticated, and so was their world. But the temptation remained to find excuses for the country's problems, and at a time when Soviet Russia was a source of confusion and anxiety, "communists" became good excuses. The inclination to blame the "reds" was strengthened at the time by several famous cases in which it appeared that communists had been involved in espionage and other dubious activities. Several Republican candidates for Congress exploited the communism issue actively, and the entire party accepted it as a welcome asset.

The red-baiting techniques first used in the 1919–20 Red Scare—when subversives were hunted by the Senate Bolshevik Investigating Committee, among many others—were revived in 1938 by Martin Dies, a Texas congressman who persuaded the House of Representatives to establish the Committee on Un-American Activities, and to make him its chairman. Dies was nominally a Democrat, but he had no sympathy for the New Deal. He decided that many New Dealers were actually dubious characters, "pinkos" and communists, and conducted a number of flamboyant "investigations" to prove it.

The committee did not function during the war, and the voters of Texas defeated Dies in 1944. But anticommunism had caught on. In 1939 Congress passed the Hatch Act, which forbade government workers to belong to any organization which owed allegiance abroad, or which advocated "violent overthrow" of the American government. In 1942, the Civil Service Commission was authorized to dismiss government employees whose loyalty was questionable. Roosevelt established the Committee of Five in 1943 to help government departments review "security risks," as suspicious people came to be known. This committee asked the attorney general's office to produce a list of "subversive organizations" for its use; groups named in the list had no legal recourse or even any official opportunity to protest. Bureaucrats in the Department of Justice had the right to decide which organizations threatened American security and which did not.

The witch-hunters were encouraged by two incidents in 1945: the *Amerasia* case and the revelation that a Russian spy ring had been operating in Canada during the war.

Amerasia was a scholarly journal of Asian affairs which supported the Chinese Communists against the Kuomintang, and defended other left-wing causes. The F.B.I. raided the magazine's offices in June 1945, and found a large number of official documents and three men employed by the government; two were foreign service officers, one was a Navy lieutenant. All three were eventually cleared, and *Amerasia*'s editor was fined $2500 for illegally possessing government papers, none of which turned out to be very sensitive. At the time of the raid, however, the incident looked like a portentous development in the rise of world communism. The publicity it received was far more impressive than the facts of the matter, and the publicity was alarming.

The Canadian spy ring was a more serious matter. An intricate network of Russians and Canadians had been gathering secret information, some of it relating to the development of atomic weapons, and sending it to Moscow. Many Americans feared that exactly the same kind of thing was going on in the United States, perhaps with the help of American officials like those involved in the *Amerasia* incident. Such fears were not entirely unjustified. They also tended to support the allegation—made in different ways by many supposedly responsible people—that there was a communist under every bed, or at least under every second one.

In late 1946, the postwar witch hunt was just beginning, though it got off to a good start. Its first targets were ill-defined categories like "New Deal radicals" and "socialists in government." Many Republican candidates in the congressional elections accepted and repeated the promise made by the party's national committee that a Republican Congress would remove the communists from government, though no one proved they were in the government at the time. Nevertheless there were numerous accusers.

In September a new magazine called *Plain Talk* first appeared, swinging a big axe at the reds and "pinkos." *Plain Talk* and other journals like it shared the barest touch of respectability, but they were joined by more formidable allies. The United States Chamber of Commerce, an organization with no history of extremism, published a booklet in early October called *Communist Infiltration in the United States,* which began a Chamber of Commerce crusade to get the reds out of influential places. According to the booklet, Communist pressures were already affecting the State Department. Francis Cardinal Spellman of New York wrote in early November, "Every communist is a potential enemy of the United States and only the bat-blind can fail to be aware of the communist invasion of our country."

The communism issue was hotly discussed that fall in intellectual circles which were not much involved in mundane issues like the meat crisis. Brooks Atkinson, *The New York Times* drama critic who had been a correspondent in Moscow, took the unusual step of devoting his regular Sunday feature article on October 6 to an attack on official Russian cultural policy and on American artists who sympathized with the Soviet Union. One of the best-selling books of 1946–47 was a bitter anti-Soviet memoir by Victor Kravchenko, a Russian official who defected to the West, called *I Chose Freedom.*

Communism was also a very important issue inside the labor movement, especially the Congress of Industrial Organizations (C.I.O.), which conducted a fierce internal debate during late 1946 on how to deal with its Communist members. (There were quite a few.) In mid-November, the C.I.O.'s Executive Council approved a firm anti-Communist declaration, but the struggle between left- and right-wing factions continued until late 1947.

Two developments during the campaign contributed to the importance of Communism in the congressional elections, the Wallace incident and a Moscow Radio broadcast on October 20. After being forced out of the Cabinet for his intemperate remarks on foreign policy—or, in the popular view, for being soft on Russia, and thus on Communism—Wallace became the model of a highly placed "Communist sympathizer." He was a much better target than the unfortunate officials who had been involved in the *Amerasia* incident; after all, he had been vice president of the United States, and closely associated with Roosevelt, the New Deal and the C.I.O.'s leftish Political Action Committee (P.A.C.). The combination was effective for those who wanted to exploit it.

If Wallace provided cause for doubts, Moscow Radio seemed to offer positive proof to some gullible Americans that a terrible conspiracy was afoot. In an English-language broadcast on October 20, a Soviet commentator advised American voters to support "progressive" candidates like those endorsed by the P.A.C., and not the reactionary Republicans. B. Carroll Reece, National Chairman of the Republican party, lost no time in wondering aloud whether the Democrats welcomed this endorsement for at least some of their candidates. John W. Bricker, an extreme right-wing Republican running for the Senate in Ohio, went further: "Definite proof has now come from Moscow that the campaign of the Political Action Committee in this country is being directed from Communist Russia," he said. The Democrats could endure exaggerations like Bricker's, but Moscow's unsolicited kind words were hardly helpful. Republicans returned to them often in the last two weeks of the campaign and with obvious success. It was generally agreed after the election results were known that "Communism" had become, in the closing weeks of the campaign, one of the four most obvious causes of the Democrats' defeat—the others being prices and shortages, labor unrest and the Wallace incident.

The issue was by no means resolved in the election. President Truman revived it in late November. Reacting to political pressure, he established the President's Temporary Commission on Employee Loyalty to review government security, and recommend whatever new action seemed appropriate. The House Committee on Un-American Activities, chaired in the Eightieth Congress by J. Parnell Thomas, a New Jersey Republican in the Dies tradition, announced a number of new investigations. John E. Rankin, a Mississippi Democrat on the committee, indicated the tone of the group's work on Christmas Day, when he said the committee planned to investigate the "pink professors" in American universities.

At the end of December a group of prominent left-wingers led by Henry Wallace established the "Progressive Citizens of America," a new political organization. It was to be the basis of the Progressive party whose banner Wallace carried in the presidential election of 1948. Less than a week later, liberal Democrats who rejected Wallace's "soft" line on Russia formed the Americans for Democratic Action. Its founders had excellent progressive credentials, but the A.D.A.'s basic tenet was anti-Communism.

In January Carl Aldo Marzani, an employee of the State Department who had worked in the Office of Strategic Services during the war, was indicted for concealing his Communist party membership. The day Marzani's indictment was announced, the State Department revealed that 3,000 recent "loyalty investigations" had produced 314 names which had required "further checking." Of those 314, 202 had left the department, 59 had been cleared of all suspicion and 53 were still being investigated. That did not sound very reassuring either. On February 6, the Un-

American Activities Committee asked the Department of Justice to bring charges against Gerhard Eisler, a German, as the leading Communist in the United States.° A revealing indication of the country's political mood that winter was a decision by the United States Court of Appeals in Chicago, which ruled that "it is libelous *per se* to write of a man or a corporation that they are Communists or Communist sympathizers."

As 1946 ended and 1947 began, Americans were becoming accustomed to charges of subversion in high places and disloyalty in all sorts of places. Such imputations became part of the political vocabulary, and were soon remarkably commonplace and acceptable. Even Robert Taft, the respected leader of the conservative wing of the Republican Party, joined those who relied on red-baiting for purposes that often had nothing to do with fighting Communism. In announcing his opposition to the appointment of David E. Lilienthal, the former director of the Tennessee Valley Authority, to the chairmanship of the Atomic Energy Commission, Taft called this progressive New Deal official "a typical power-hungry bureaucrat ... temperamentally unfitted to head any important executive agency in a democratic government, and too soft on issues connected with Communism and Soviet Russia." Taft's statement followed a long Senate hearing on Lilienthal's nomination in which the nominee was repeatedly accused of sympathizing with Communism.°° The Lilienthal case was one of the biggest news stories in America in February 1947, when Britain was shivering in the dark.

The importance of Communism as a subject for worry or something worse continued to grow after the election and

° Also in February, President Truman received the first F.B.I. report based on the "revelations" of Elizabeth Bentley and Whittaker Chambers implicating Harry Dexter White, Alger Hiss and others. But these celebrated cases did not come to the public's attention until the summer of 1948.
°°These charges were apparently contrived by Sen. Kenneth McKellar, a bitter old man of 78 who had disliked Lilienthal since he had refused to appoint McKellar's friends and cronies to jobs with the T.V.A.

throughout 1947, but some of the other problems which had made 1946 so difficult began to disappear after the November elections. Meat reappeared in the grocery stores, and people were soon eating more of it than ever before. Newspapers began to grow fat with advertisements for consumer goods; car production and the level of manufacturing generally went up quickly. Conversations about new televisions and ballpoint pens replaced the complaints about meat so often heard just months before. A few days after the congressional elections, President Truman removed all remaining wage and price controls except those on rents, rice and sugar. On New Year's Eve he declared that World War II was legally ended, thereby rescinding several wartime taxes and restrictions. Some wartime regulations remained in force, but many more were removed in February.

The labor situation improved, too, although for a time just after the election, it looked as though the unions might become more, not less, troublesome. John L. Lewis kept a promise he made in late October, and made plans for a miners' strike on November 20 unless the government agreed to reopen negotiations with the miners. Truman was furious, and sought a court injunction to stop the strike. (An injunction would have been illegal in normal times, but because the government was running the mines, it was possible then.) The injunction was granted, but Lewis and his men went on strike anyhow.

Lewis was promptly cited for contempt of court. He challenged the charge, and chose to face trial. When his trial began, the strike was already ten days old, rail travel was restricted by the government to save coal, and many cities had reduced electricity production to wartime levels. The dramatic trial in a crowded Washington courtroom lasted for two days, and when the lawyers had finished their presentations (no witnesses appeared) the presiding judge found Lewis in contempt of court. He was fined $10,000, and the United Mine Workers was fined the remarkable sum of $3,500,000. Both refused to pay, and Lewis appealed to the Supreme Court.

Four days later, on Saturday, December 7, the White House announced that President Truman would speak on the radio to the nation that night, asking the miners to disregard Lewis and return to work. That afternoon, Lewis called a press conference. Because, he said, the Supreme Court should be allowed to judge his appeal "free from public pressure superinduced by the hysteria of an economic crisis," he was ending the strike.

It was an important victory for President Truman. Clark Clifford, his closest aide in the White House at the time, recalled many years later that the confrontation with Lewis was "the moment when Truman finally and irrevocably stepped out from the shadow of F.D.R. to become president in his own right . . . There was a big difference . . . from then on. He was his own boss."

Truman knew the public was disturbed by his previous efforts to solve major labor problems, and he knew also that John L. Lewis's November strike had no significant popular support. It was a good opportunity to get tough, and he did, with the best possible results. The record of the Truman presidency suggests that the president fancied himself a "fighter," and after his combat with Lewis, he appeared to be so. Truman recovered both his composure and the political initiative before Congress returned to Washington in January.

On January 6, Truman went to the House of Representatives to deliver the State of the Union address. His opening remarks concerned the problems of a president of one party trying to work with a Congress controlled by the other. No doubt, he said, they would differ on some questions, but they should be able to agree on many. Constructive cooperation was absolutely necessary—without it, "we shall be risking the nation's safety and destroying our own opportunities for progress." In fact, Truman had decided not to yield even slightly to the new Congress and the "conservatism" it represented.

The program he first outlined more than a year before in his September 6, 1945, speech remained almost intact. He wanted a big housing program, assistance for small businessmen, an expensive farm program, health insurance for everyone, a new cabinet-level Department of Welfare and a balanced budget achieved not just by reducing spending, but by temporarily retaining some wartime taxes. He said labor disputes were an important problem, and new legislation was necessary, but "we must not, in order to punish a few labor leaders, pass vindictive laws which will restrict the proper rights of the rank and file of labor."

Two days later, in his Economic Report to Congress, Truman reviewed the economic situation and its implications for the year ahead. Despite recent improvements in many branches of the economy, Truman was not optimistic. Prices were still going up, industrial investment was not increasing as fast as hoped, and there remained "a backlog of unsatisfied wants, especially for housing, commercial construction, automobiles, household appliances, furnishings and other durable goods."

In neither message did Truman even mention what Republican congressional leaders wanted most to hear—that big reductions in government spending, especially on New Deal programs, were planned. The Republicans had grandiose ideas; some suggested that $10 billion ought to be cut from the next budget, others wanted to save $3–6 billion. Truman only said that spending would have to be carefully watched, and the budget balanced. (It was.)

Despite the opposition of a Republican Congress, the government in Washington seemed much more settled in the first months of 1947 than it had during the previous year. Truman deserved some credit for the change; he had become more careful, more deliberate. A general improvement in economic conditions helped him. After Truman's fight with Lewis, strikes were less common. Incomes rose, production increased and the standard of living improved steadily, even if prices continued to climb. Important weaknesses persisted, especially in the construction industry, but there was some cause for optimism.

America had come through a period of great strain and immense frustrations. Expectations for the postwar world had been wildly optimistic, and realities were depressingly complicated. But by early 1947, the public had generally accepted those realities, and conditions were improving. The big news stories in January and February were new accusations and revelations about security risks in the government, and the Lilienthal controversy. Meat crises and coal strikes were mercifully forgotten. People did not worry as much, or complain as often—except perhaps about international affairs, but that was another matter.

CHAPTER III

"All the world is in trouble at once;
the troubles do not come one at a
time."
—Ernest Bevin, *the British Foreign
Secretary, February 27, 1947.*

I n Britain and America, the domestic politics of 1946–47 were
chaotic. Troubles at home devoured the time and energies of
the leaders of both countries. But as Ernest Bevin ruefully
observed in the House of Commons in February 1947, the outside
world refused to stand aside for domestic crises.

Ideally, the postwar world would have been much calmer. If
events had conformed to the optimism epitomized by Franklin D.
Roosevelt's diplomacy, 1946 would have been a year of orderly
adjustment to peace within the framework of a new United Nations organization. The realities of power politics quickly super-
seded that kind of optimism, and the realities of postwar politics
were sadly straightforward: the alliance that defeated Nazi Germany and Japan did not survive, because its members' interests
quickly diverged once the war was won.

In retrospect this was not surprising. At various times during
the war Britain, America and the Soviet Union each tried to create
the impression of an overriding common interest shared by all
three, but this interest never really existed. The diplomatic and
personal records of the war that are now available all reveal an
alliance of convenience, in which Britain and America shared

intimate relations (though even they were sometimes perverted by mutual suspicion), and Soviet Russia played the odd-man-out.

Some historians have argued that this unnatural relationship made a cold war or something like it inevitable. If it were really possible to attribute inevitabilities to history, this might be true. But it is misleading to think that the politicians in Britain and America believed that a hostile confrontation with the Soviet Union was unavoidable after the war. They believed nothing of the kind. Officials in Washington and London watched with dismay as the Soviet Union took increasingly independent and self-centered positions on virtually every issue of postwar diplomacy.

Not that the Anglo-Saxon allies expected Stalin to live up to the lofty sentiments of the Atlantic Charter, the declaration of self-determination for all people and self-effacement for all nations which provided a rhetorical basis for the American war effort. During the war Churchill and (less willingly) Roosevelt acquiesced to Stalin's claims for territory: the Baltic states, plus slices of Finland, Rumania and Poland. They acknowledged too that postwar states in Eastern Europe would have to cooperate with their Soviet neighbor.

There is evidence that Stalin interpreted this acquiescence as a sign that the British and Americans would give him a completely free hand in all of Eastern Europe, and perhaps even beyond, but this assumption was never justified. Perhaps naively, but for all of that no less firmly, the Americans and British both felt that the Soviet Union's rights in Eastern Europe were limited. Moreover and more important, Roosevelt (and therefore many important Americans) believed that by acquiescing to limited Soviet demands in Eastern Europe and especially in Poland, he was assuring Stalin's cooperation in more important matters—making peace and establishing the United Nations. Churchill personally was more cynical and less hopeful, but in both Britain and America, the informed citizens who led public opinion, the politicians and the major newspapers all expected the postwar world to evolve more harmoniously than it did.

Instead of harmony, relations between the Soviet Union and the Anglo-Saxon allies were marked by nastiness and contention from the end of the war through 1946. The British and Americans blamed Soviet intransigence for this. Soviet behavior after the war made a crucial contribution to the political atmosphere in Britain and the United States which made the cold war possible.

That is not to say that the collapse of the alliance and subsequent confrontations between East and West were entirely the responsibility of the Soviet Union. Exploiting the immeasurable advantages of hindsight, recent histories have demonstrated that the Americans (and to a lesser extent the British) were naive to expect to substitute a United Nations and high-sounding principles for power politics and spheres of influence. Had Russian insecurities and historical imperatives been better understood at the time, postwar expectations might have been more modest. In the event, British and American policies probably added to the tense postwar atmosphere. By word and deed (and often by mistake), Britain and America undoubtedly compounded the anxieties which motivated Soviet policy.

In the international politics of 1946–47, Britain and America believed that they were being fair and reasonable; they believed they were adhering to international agreements. Though small, left-wing groups in both countries argued that the Soviet Union should be appeased, the leaders of the major British and American political parties disagreed. During 1946–47, these politicians believed the Russians were the troublemakers.·

The single best statement of frustration with Soviet behavior was a memorandum prepared in September 1946, for President Truman by one of his closest associates, Clark M. Clifford. In his memorandum Clifford compiled a resumé of every important agreement which—in the official American view—the Soviet Union had violated since the end of the war.° It took 5000 words to enumerate them all—dozens of specific instances.

° Clifford's memorandum is reprinted in full in Arthur Krock's *Memoirs: Sixty Years on the Firing Line,* 1968.

Clifford acknowledged that there was ambiguity in the deteriorating relationship with the Soviet Union. "Many of the acts of the Soviet government appear to the United States government to be violations of the spirit of an international agreement," he wrote, "although it is difficult to adduce direct evidence of literal violations." Clifford noted two Soviet maneuvers used to avoid literal violations. One was to define words like "democracy" and "fascist" in terms that contradicted American definitions of those words. The second was to compel governments in Eastern Europe to violate international agreements to help the Soviets pursue their own interests without breaking agreements themselves.

The implicit theme of Clifford's analysis was that for Moscow, national interests prevailed over any treaty, agreement or understanding. Sometimes the Soviet Union expressed this single-mindedness subtly, sometimes baldly.

In some cases, Clifford wrote, the Soviet Union had simply ignored agreements: for example, when it installed a government in Austria without consulting Britain and America, contrary to Allied understandings. In other cases Moscow said one thing but did another—agreeing to demilitarize Germany, for instance, while keeping open German defense plants to equip Soviet forces. Other violations seemed to be deliberate harassments. For example, the Soviet Union offered little or no help to the American prisoners of war that the Red Army liberated in Poland, and refused to let American planes pick them up from Odessa when (usually by their own devices) they finally reached that Soviet port.

Clifford's review covered events through the first half of 1946. Subsequent developments reinforced the frustrations he reported. In late 1946 and early 1947, Britain and the United States shared a series of experiences at international conferences and in diplomatic disputes which strengthened the conviction that they could no longer hope for a postwar peace governed jointly by the Allies that won the war.

The first four meetings of the Allied Council of Foreign Ministers after the war achieved little. The American Secretary of State, James F. Byrnes, allowed the first to end inconclusively and in failure in October 1945, rather than concede to the Soviet Union that France should have no voice in the deliberations on peace in Eastern Europe. Britain's Foreign Secretary, Ernest Bevin, supported Byrnes's decision. In December 1945, the council met again in Moscow. The Big Three appeared then to agree on several issues, thanks largely to American concessions, but each agreement eventually proved to be superficial. Two further sessions in Paris during the summer of 1946 led to the twenty-one-nation Paris Peace Conference. The Big Three, France, China and sixteen countries which had signed armistice agreements with Bulgaria, Finland, Hungary, Italy and Rumania were invited to the conference. These last five nations were the former German satellites. The goal of the conference was to write a formal peace treaty for each of them. The German and Austrian treaties, which were expected to take more time, were not on the agenda.

To persuade the Soviet Union to participate in the Peace Conference, Britain and the United States agreed to require Italy to pay reparations of $100 million to the Soviet Union. That was an immense amount for the impoverished Italians, and much more than Byrnes or Bevin wanted to ask of them. However, the Russians also made a concession. Before the Peace Conference began, they agreed that Trieste should be put under some kind of international control, rather than under the control of Yugoslavia, Russia's ally, or Italy. These were the only significant agreements the Allies had reached eleven months after Japan's surrender.

The reason so little progress had been made was obvious—to the American side. The Soviet Union consistently found British and American proposals unacceptable, on almost all topics. In a radio broadcast in July 1946, Secretary Byrnes told the American people, "I sometimes think our Soviet friends fear we would think them weak and soft if they agreed without a struggle to anything we wanted, even if they wanted it too." The remark seemed valid, regardless of whether Byrnes and Bevin had alienated the Russians. Few people in Britain or America thought they had. In both countries, it was the Russians who appeared unreasonable. Soviet representatives at various meetings repeatedly took up more time in debate than any of their colleagues; they continually disputed the most insignificant questions of procedure; and they invariably refused to accept any Anglo-American suggestion until they had modified it in at least some small way.

The Paris Peace Conference convened on July 29, 1946. It began with a long fight on procedure; precisely, on which of the conference's decisions would be recommended to the Council of Foreign Ministers. (The council would write the final treaties.) The Soviet Union feared, perhaps with reason, that Britain and America would try to dictate solutions to many questions facing the conference, and insisted that only the suggestions approved by a two-thirds vote be recommended to the foreign ministers. Britain and the United States, supported by many of the smaller nations, thought a simple majority should be enough. After a week of haggling, the dispute was resolved by a British compromise: the conference would make two kinds of recommendations to the council, those approved by a simple majority and those passed by two-thirds. The compromise was accepted by fifteen votes to six. The Soviet Union, Czechoslovakia, Poland, the Ukraine, Belorussia and Yugoslavia voted against. It was to become a familiar alignment.

At Byrnes's urging, meetings of the nine commissions into which the conference was divided were open to the press. Apparently, the secretary of state wanted to demonstrate as clearly as possible why making peace was so difficult. He thought press coverage would make it clear to world opinion which side was holding up peacemaking efforts. Byrnes's stratagem was partially successful, but it also had an unfortunate effect. Knowing that their remarks were being recorded and published, delegates from all countries became as interested in scoring points with international public opinion as in solving the problems at hand. Propaganda, much of it attacking Britain and America, became a regular feature of the conference. Reporters in Paris, especially American and British correspondents, began looking for signs of an East-West split, and they found many in the harsh words exchanged between Soviet delegates and their allies and the delegates from most of the other fifteen participating countries.

Though the atmosphere of the conference was not congenial, some work was accomplished. Three issues most concerned the delegates: the total amount of reparations to be exacted from the former German satellites; control of the Danube; and control of Trieste. No agreement was reached on the reparations question. On September 24, the Big Four decided that the conference was proceeding too slowly, and agreed that October 15 be set as adjournment date to try to speed its deliberations. In the remaining three weeks, the conference did make substantial progress on both the Danube and Trieste questions. Hundreds of smaller items were also considered, and when the conference ended on October 15, fifty-three proposals had been approved by two-thirds of the participants, and forty-one others by simple majorities.

The deadline proved to be a successful gambit. Unless the reparations issue really was insoluble, there seemed no reason why the five minor treaties could not be completed quickly. The Council of Foreign Ministers met in New York on November 4 to try to draft final agreements. The meeting started very smoothly. Soviet foreign minister Molotov made no trouble on procedural questions. But when substantive discussions began, Molotov tried to reopen all the most controversial questions debated in Paris, especially that of Trieste. The Russian foreign minister ignored the recommendations of the Peace Conference, whether approved by two-thirds of the delegates or not. After several weeks of frustrating exchanges, Molotov approached Byrnes and asked how they could make better progress. Byrnes replied that because Molotov had rejected all the Peace Conference's recommendations, "I see no hope for agreement." He said that he had come to the conclusion "that we will not be able to agree upon the treaties. Having become reconciled to this," he went on, "I think we should agree to disagree without having any of the bitter exchanges that marked some of the debates at Paris."

Molotov said he was not so pessimistic; he thought there was a better chance of reaching an agreement. Two days later, he startled the other foreign ministers by taking a much more conciliatory line on several subjects. Soon the Four were able to agree on one issue, then another and another. In less than two weeks the five treaties were written, and seventy-seven of the recommendations of the Paris Conference (including forty-seven of those approved by two-thirds votes) had been accepted by the foreign ministers. There was no doubt in American minds, at least, that Byrnes's firm line with Molotov made the difference. This explanation was leaked to the press at the time.

Before adjourning, the council agreed to meet again in Moscow in March 1947, to begin considering the German and Austrian treaties. The Four decided to send deputies to Paris to prepare for the March meeting. These meetings, which continued through January and most of February, produced only a few minor agreements on the Austrian treaty and a long list of disagreements about Germany which divided the Western allies from the Soviet Union.

Debates at the United Nations in the fall and winter of 1946–47 were even less productive than the various peace conferences. The United Nations had first met in January 1946. It considered several controversies, but had not yet made a significant contribution to peace or international political cooperation when the Security Council reconvened at Lake Success, New York, on August 28, 1946.

From August until the following spring, the topics which most concerned the major powers at the United Nations were Greece, the admission of new members, problems of disarmament and peacekeeping and—in the Atomic Energy Commission—international control of nuclear energy. (This last debate will be discussed in Chapter V.)

The periodic debates on the applications of countries wishing to join the United Nations occasionally produced new members, but during 1946–47, many of them ended without result. The prob'·m was most obvious in late September, when Russia vetoed the applications of Eire, Portugal, and Transjordan, and Britain and America vetoed Outer Mongolia and Albania. The presumptuous attitude of both the Soviet Union and the Western allies upset many smaller nations, several of whom pressed for a debate on abuses of the veto power. They were clearly afraid that hostility between East and West might make Great Power unanimity a practical impossibility. The Security Council debated the veto for several weeks but got nowhere. In November, the council referred the question back to the General Assembly.

Greece's problems were debated on several occasions during 1946. It had become a favorite subject of the Soviet Union and her allies, who used it as a reply to criticism of their own policies. In late August 1946, the Ukraine complained to the Security Council that Greece was seeking a war with Albania, was persecuting Slavic and Albanian minorities in her northern provinces, and was a general threat to the peace—and that Britain was ultimately responsible for all these transgressions. (British troops were then stationed in Greece, and had fought briefly on the side of Conservative government forces against Communist rebels in October 1944.) Britain and the United States rejected each accusation. The ensuing debate led nowhere, and the Ukraine's complaint was dropped from the Security Council's agenda on September 20.

In December Greece itself revived the issue by complaining that her northern neighbors, Yugoslavia, Bulgaria and Albania, were supporting the rebels operating in northern Greece. The council agreed on December 19 to send a commission to investigate the Greek situation. It was the United Nation's most substantial achievement of the year. When the United States first proposed such a commission several months earlier, the Soviet

Union opposed it. In December the Russians apparently decided that they could use the commission to publicize the excesses of the right-wing Greek regime.

The United Nations charter established a Military Staff Committee, composed of the permanent members of the Security Council, to advise the secretary general on the organization's peacekeeping force. The committee met in desultory fashion throughout the first half of 1946. Its first task was to "formulate recommendations ... as to the basic principles which should govern the organizations of the United Nations forces." A subcommittee was formed to establish a method by which member nations could contribute to the U.N. force. Neither group had any success. During a debate on disarmament in December, the General Assembly asked the Security Council to "accelerate as much as possible the placing at its disposal of the armed forces mentioned in Article 43 of the Charter." In response, the Security Council asked the Military Staff Committee in February to reexamine the principles which might be the basis of a U.N. force.

The Staff Committee's debate revealed that on all fundamental questions, Britain and the United States were of one opinion, while the Soviet Union was of another. Russia favored the principle of "equal contributions," meaning that no nation could give more than the contribution of the smallest member of the United Nations. Britain and America thought this was utterly unrealistic. Russia thought the troops contributed to the United Nations should be left at home until they were needed; Britain and America wanted them stationed together at all times. Forty-one principles were proposed in these meetings. There was disagreement on sixteen of them.

The joint Allied occupation of Germany never worked smoothly. From the start the Soviet Union took a different approach to the German problem from Britain and the United States. (France, too, disagreed with the Anglo-Saxons, for her own reasons.)

Throughout 1946 the Allied Control Commission tried to find some basis for an agreement among the Big Four on Germany's future, but without success. Britain and the United States received regular reports of disturbing events in the Soviet zone: of scientists kidnaped, soldiers conscripted into the Red Army, and Nazi politicians pardoned for their past associations if they joined the Socialist Unity Party (S.E.D.), Germany's Communist party. Though the Potsdam agreements specifically stipulated that the occupying powers should treat all of Germany as a single economic unit, the Soviets refused to do this. Instead, they exacted enormous reparations from their zone of occupation.

In April 1946, Secretary Byrnes formally proposed a new treaty to the Big Four that would have guaranteed the demilitarization of Germany for twenty-five years. The Americans hoped this formula would reassure the Soviet Union that it need not act out of fear of any future German threat.* Immediately after Byrnes made this suggestion, the United States cut off delivery of reparations shipments from its zone to the Soviet zone, both because it disapproved of the Soviet policy of removing reparations before agreement on a peace treaty, and because the United States hoped to persuade the Soviets and the French to accept that Germany was a single economic unit.

Stopping the delivery of reparations was America's first overtly hostile act directed against the Soviet Union, but the Russians apparently thought it was a bluff, and made no great issue of it.

The Russians were not so sanguine in July, when the United States announced its willingness to merge the American zone of occupation with any other zone or zones for economic and administrative efficiency. This was a reaction to further American frustration over the Allies' inability to agree on occupation policy. To Britain, which could ill afford the expenses of maintaining its

---

* Sen. Arthur Vandenberg of Michigan, the Republican spokesman on foreign affairs and a member of Byrnes's delegation when this treaty was proposed, recorded in his diary at the time: "If and when Molotov [V.M. Molotov, the Soviet foreign minister] finally refuses this offer, he will confess that he wants *expansion* and not 'security.' "

zone, the American proposal must have looked attractive on economic grounds alone. On July 29 Britain agreed in principle to a merger, and began talks with the Americans to work out details. Several days later, the Soviet representative on the Allied Control Council for Germany described the British decision as "unwise."

The Soviet press attacked this new Anglo-American arrangement—known as "Bizonia"—with a vehemence that surprised even the Foreign Office in London. This was the first instance when any of the wartime Allies had acted independently of the others on a question of central importance to all of them. After Bizonia, the pretense of a common Allied policy in Europe could no longer be maintained.*

On September 6, Secretary Byrnes made inter-Allied differences clearer in what was symbolically one of the most important speeches of the postwar era. His speech was in part a reply to a statement by Molotov in July that Russia favored a strong and united Germany—pleasing words to German ears. At Stuttgart, Byrnes said that America, too, favored a united and prosperous Germany, and that America did not regard the Oder as Germany's final eastern frontier. (Russia did; the boundary had been provisionally accepted at Potsdam.)

Byrnes promised that "as long as an occupation force is required in Germany the army of the United States will be part of that occupation force." He criticized the Allied Control Council for its inability to agree on a program to unify and strengthen the German nation. "If complete unification cannot be secured, we shall do everything in our power to secure maximum possible unification," Byrnes added. This meant he had abandoned previous U.S. policy. Six weeks later, Bevin said the British government was "in almost complete agreement" with everything Byrnes said.

---

* Some historians have suggested that the cancellation of reparations deliveries in May was the decisive act splitting the wartime Allies. This is an exaggeration, as any such generalization must be. A *rapprochement* could have been possible even after May 1946. And the United States, at least, thought the dispute with Russia over Iran in March 1946, was much more important than the cessation of reparations shipments in Germany.

The United States and Britain tried to convince the Soviet Union that Bizonia was neither a political alignment nor a final arrangement. The purpose of establishing it was to remove all economic barriers between the two zones, and to pool imports and natural resources to achieve a common standard of living. Germans joined British and American officials on five planning boards to establish economic policy for the principal sectors of Bizonia's economy, but these boards were deliberately headquartered in five different cities to avoid the creation of one "capital" or the impression that Bizonia was in any way a government. Bevin told the House of Commons in February that since Bizonia's inception, "in order that Germany should not be divided into halves, or Europe divided into halves, we have made it clear that it was open to the other two powers to join in [Bizonia], on the assumption that each would make a fair contribution to the cost of running Germany. . . ." He made it quite plain that Britain had joined America to form Bizonia to save money, and not for political reasons, though he certainly understood the political implications.

Relations among the Allies in Germany worsened steadily throughout 1946. Contentious propaganda began to appear in the newspapers of the British, American and Soviet zones in the second half of the year. (Most of the papers were controlled by the occupying powers.) When Marshal Sokolovsky, the Russian representative on the Council, complained of an article in a British-zone paper in late August, America's representative, General Lucius Clay, replied bitterly that the story would be investigated if the marshal would in turn investigate half a dozen recent stories in Soviet-zone newspapers which accused Britain and America of a variety of sins, including the charge that American officials had been "friends" of Hitler. This exchange led to an agreement to stop propaganda attacks—an agreement which lasted one month.

In October residents of Berlin elected a new city government, and apparently surprised the Soviet occupation authorities in the process. The Social Democratic Party won the election with 48.7 percent of the vote; Christian Democrats were second with 22 percent. The Communist S.E.D. was third with only 19.8 percent of the vote, "although encouraged in East Berlin in every possible way by the Soviet military administration," according to General Clay. A few days later, Stalin told an American reporter that on the basis of recent election results, he was "not satisfied" that Germany was developing "democratically."

In February the Oberbuergermeister chosen by the Social Democrats was forced by his own party to resign because he was too accommodating with the Russians. Ernst Reuter, a former Communist who had become bitterly anti-Soviet, was chosen to succeed him, but Russian protests made it impossible for him to take office, and an acting mayor was appointed. A Soviet general, P.A. Kurochkin, commented that the Social Democrats' selection of Reuter "should serve as a warning ... of the undesirability of hasty abatement of [Allied] control. ..."

The Allied Control Council, like the foreign ministers' deputies in Paris, tried in early 1947 to find some common ground on which the foreign ministers could base their discussions in Moscow in March. As in Paris, the British and American position was irreconcilable with the Russian view. The three could not even agree on a description of what had happened in Germany since the Nazi surrender, let alone on a policy for the future.

Germany was not the only country in which the Soviet Union appeared to be saying one thing but doing quite another during 1946. Britain and the United States both believed that throughout Eastern Europe, in almost every country the Red Army had liberated in 1945, the Russians were ignoring the principles of the Yalta Declaration on Liberated Europe—sometimes systematically, sometimes quite casually.

The British and American attitudes toward Eastern Europe were ambivalent. Neither government could pretend that postwar events in the countries along the Soviet border were completely unexpected. At Teheran in 1943, Churchill and Roosevelt had acknowledged a Soviet upper hand in Poland. In Moscow in late

1944, Churchill had proposed to Stalin a division of influence in much of Eastern Europe. Churchill suggested that Soviet-British predominance be divided 90–10 in Rumania, 75–25 in Bulgaria, 50–50 in Yugoslavia and Hungary, and 10–90 (in Britain's favor, in other words) in Greece. Stalin agreed. Roosevelt and Churchill both accepted the inevitability of Soviet predominance in the region, if only because neither was prepared to challenge the Red Army, which occupied these countries.

But diplomacy is a game of appearances as well as substance. Appearances can be even more important than reality. The Americans, especially, were anxious to preserve the appearance that Eastern Europe was being allowed a significant degree of self-determination after the war. Roosevelt took the Yalta Declaration on Liberated Europe seriously because it satisfied his political needs at the time. He explained repeatedly to Stalin that for reasons of domestic American politics (*i.e.*, largely to satisfy Americans of Eastern European origin), the Eastern European countries had to be given the appearance of self-determination.

Moreover, neither the British nor the Americans believed that by acknowledging Eastern Europe's position in a Soviet sphere of influence they were relinquishing these countries to rigid, Soviet-style dictatorships. The traditional definition of a sphere of influence was an area in which one power's ultimate desires held sway. This was a far cry from the thorough control of both domestic and foreign policies which the Soviet Union seemed to demand in Eastern Europe. Stalin's roughshod seizure of control, his uncompromising attitude and the brazenness of Soviet policy all alarmed the Anglo-Saxon allies.

Of all the Eastern European countries, Poland attracted the most attention. Poland had been a principal topic of discussion among the Big Three for years, and the subject was thoroughly reviewed at Yalta. Britain and America agreed at Yalta to recognize the Soviet-sponsored Lublin regime, provided it was broadened to include several representatives of more popular groups, including Stanislaw Mikolajczyk, premier of the government in exile which functioned in London during the war. In return, Stalin promised speedy and free elections. And he signed the Declaration on Liberated Europe, thus agreeing on paper that provisional regimes should be established in Eastern Europe "broadly representative of all democratic elements in the population and pledged to the earliest possible establishment through free elections of governments responsive to the will of the people."

As soon as Britain and the United States recognized the Soviet-dominated Polish regime, the strong Communist element began to consolidate its position. A referendum was held in June to approve the government's policy of nationalization, its decision to consider the Oder-Neisse line a final western frontier, and the abolition of the upper house of the Polish legislature. All three carried, but Mikolajczyk protested that the vote was a fraud. In August Britain and America sent notes to the Polish regime criticizing ballot counting in the referendum and questioning the suppression of the two largest political parties in the country. Both notes asked for assurances that the general election (for which a date would be set in November) would be absolutely free. Poland rejected both notes, calling them interference in its domestic affairs. Soon afterward, the British government said it would hold $16 million (£4 million) in Polish gold reserves on deposit in London until free elections were held.

During the autumn it became obvious that the Polish regime was preparing for a decisive, if not convincing, electoral victory. Popular political leaders were harassed and often imprisoned; in six weeks of October and November, four of the leaders of the Polish Peasant Party were arrested. Just before the election date was set, Britain and the United States delivered notes to the Polish government recalling its commitment, first made at Yalta, to "free and unfettered elections." The notes were ignored, and January 19 was chosen as election day. As the day approached, terrorism became blatant and widespread, and it was vividly publicized in the West. Before election day the United States sent (and published) a note to Britain and the Soviet Union, asking that they protest together against terrorism and the suppression of political activity in Poland. A week later, Moscow Radio rejected the suggestion.

Polling day was violent. About thirty people were killed. The government and its supporters won 398 of the 444 seats in the parliament. Mikolajczyk's Peasant Party won only twenty-four seats, a low number even in those circumstances. A few days later, Mikolajczyk announced that at every polling place where his party was allowed to post an observer, his candidate was elected, but where there was no Peasant Party pollwatcher, it was invariably defeated. British and American officials in Warsaw were persuaded by Mikolajczyk and their own observations that the election was not a free one. Notes reporting this view to the Poles were soon sent from London and Washington. Early in February 1947, Christopher Mayhew, parliamentary secretary of the Foreign Office, explained the British view of the election in the House of Commons:

> The powers of the Polish Provisional Government were extensively used to reduce to a minimum the vote of those opposed to the Government *bloc*. Opposition lists of candidates in areas covering 22 percent of the electorate were completely suppressed. Candidates' and voters' names were removed from the lists; candidates were arrested; Government officials, members of the armed forces and many others were made to vote openly.... The count was conducted in conditions entirely controlled by the government *bloc*....

Britain and the United States did not break diplomatic relations with the Poles, but soon after the election both recalled their ambassadors for consultation. (Neither ever returned to Warsaw.) Governments dominated by Communists in Bulgaria and Rumania entrenched themselves after similarly dubious elections several months earlier, also over the objections of the United States and Britain. These two Baltic states had been the subject of a compromise at the Moscow meeting of foreign ministers in December 1945. At that time the Soviet Union promised that the Bulgarian and Rumanian regimes would be broadened to include representatives of non-Communist parties, and that free elections would soon be held.

On the basis of these promises, Britain and America recognized Rumania in February 1946. But in the months that followed, there was no evidence that the democratization promised at Moscow was being implemented. Britain and America protested twice to this effect during 1946. Elections were scheduled for November 1946, and as they approached, both Britain and America objected that opposition parties were not receiving fair treatment. America made the last such protest two days before the election, to no avail. Pro-government candidates won more than 90 percent of the seats in Rumania's parliament.

Bulgaria never made even a gesture to comply with the Moscow promises. The only candidates permitted to run in the Bulgarian election of November 1945 supported the regime. Britain and the United States refused to recognize the government in Sofia, but protested nevertheless against the preparations it made for another election in October 1946. Several days before polling day, the United States, with Britain's support, suggested that the Big Three supervise the election. The Soviet Union refused, describing such supervision as "meddling" in Bulgaria's internal affairs. The result of the voting was a new parliament of 366 progovernment deputies and 99 from opposition parties. Britain and the United States continued to refuse to recognize Bulgaria until February 1947, when they signed the Bulgarian peace treaty.

Albania angered Britain and America by renouncing all of its treaty obligations after the war, and by making life increasingly difficult and uncomfortable for American and British diplomats in Tirana. The British government announced in April 1946, that the minister-designate to Albania would be kept at home, and no Albanian envoy to London would be received. In November the United States withdrew its delegation from Tirana. Throughout

1946 the Albanian government drew closer to its Communist-dominated neighbors and to the Soviet Union. (The government's own position had been established in an election at the end of 1945, when only government supporters were allowed to run.)

British-Albanian relations became hostile after October 22, 1946, when mines in the Corfu Channel off Albania blew up a British ship, killing forty-five people. Repeated British protests and a two-week "ultimatum" in mid-December all failed to elicit even an apology from the Albanians, who suggested that Greece or even Britain itself had mined the Channel. According to the Albanian government, British ships were only allowed in the Channel if they were on an "innocent passage," and the damaged ship was on a more nefarious mission. The United Nations considered the dispute in January and February, but it dragged on unresolved for years. (The World Court decided in April 1949 that Albania should pay damages to Britain.)

Anglo-American relations with Yugoslavia were even worse. Marshal Tito had first been troublesome in 1945, when Churchill and Truman decided that Yugoslav troops had to be kept out of Trieste and most of the surrounding area of Venezia Giulia. Britain and the United States had recognized Tito's regime in December 1945, a month after elections in which his national front won 90 percent of the vote. But relations were never friendly, and the three countries quarreled repeatedly. Venezia Giulia and Trieste remained sensitive areas.

In late March 1946, Britain and the United States thought it necessary to warn Tito against invading Zone A, the western half of Venezia Giulia occupied by Anglo-American troops. In May Britain and America denied that they were threatening Yugoslav sovereignty, and criticized the behavior of Yugoslav soldiers in their Zone B of Venezia Giulia. The same notes accused Marshal Tito personally of distorting the facts, and charged Yugoslavia with nine different "provocations." In July, four Yugoslav soldiers were killed in Venezia Giulia. Tito blamed the incident on the United States.

On August 9 a United States C-47 transport plane lost in a storm while flying supplies from Vienna to Undine in northern Italy flew below thick clouds to get a bearing and found itself over Yugoslavia, near Ljubljana. Two Yugoslav fighters fired on the C-47 and forced it to the ground, firing even after it crashed to earth, according to American officials. The pilot and copilot were injured and the plane was badly damaged. American diplomats were not permitted to see the crew and passengers, all of whom were held in prison.

Ten days later, a second C-47 flying the same route was shot down and all five men aboard were killed. The same day, Tito rejected the American version of the August 9 incident—that the plane was on an innocent flight to move supplies—and protested against the "constant and systematic flights of U.S. military aircraft over Yugoslavia." He said Yugoslavia wanted peace, "but not at any price." Britain and the United States released the notes they had sent Yugoslavia in May and August, "cracking the situation wide open," as one journalist put it. In Washington, Undersecretary of State Dean Acheson called the incident "an outrageous performance," and in Venezia Giulia, 10,000 British and American troops paraded next to the Morgan Line which divided Zones A and B. The American joint chiefs of staff let it be known that they were considering the implications of the attacks with British military representatives in Washington.

The day after the second plane was shot down, Byrnes met Yugoslavia's Vice Premier, Edward Kardelj, in Paris (both were attending the Peace Conference) and asked for an explanation of the attacks on American airplanes. Kardelj had "no information" about the incident; Byrnes asked him to get some. He then cabled Acheson in Washington, instructing him to draft a cable for the American ambassador in Belgrade to deliver to Tito. It was the strongest protest yet made in the postwar period.

The United States demanded that Yugoslavia recant "these outrageous acts" which were "shocking to the American people" by immediately freeing the crew and passengers of the attacked planes and guaranteeing their free passage out of Yugoslavia. It also demanded that American diplomats be allowed to communicate with the prisoners. If Yugoslavia did not comply within forty-eight hours, "the United States Government will call upon the Security Council of the United Nations to take appropriate action." At 8 A.M. on August 22, the nine men Yugoslavia had held were sent over the Morgan Line into Allied Venezia Giulia. Later, Tito announced that he had ordered his air force not to fire on foreign planes. The United States decided that he had complied with the ultimatum, but reserved its right to go to the United Nations.

The Americans were confident that they knew who had encouraged Yugoslavia to take its bold step in the first place, then to retreat. Byrnes had seen Molotov and Kardelj talking together just after the news of the U.S. ultimatum had reached Paris, and he "suspected what they were discussing." Apparently, Britain and the United States thought the C-47 incident was a test of their resolve. They feared that a sudden attempt to seize Trieste might have followed a conciliatory reaction to the aircraft attacks.* But the Western Allies were not conciliatory. The next flight from Vienna to Undine, on August 26, was not made by an unarmed C-47, but by a B-29 bomber with guns and gunners.

Czechoslovakia and Hungary were the only East European countries which were not clearly within the Soviet orbit at the beginning of 1947. But the Czechs had aggravated Secretary Byrnes by openly taking the Soviet side of almost every question at the Paris Peace Conference. When he saw a Czech delegate applaud a Russian's attack on "dollar imperialism" in Paris in October, Byrnes angrily decided to suspend $40 million of a $50

---

* John C. Campbell, who worked closely with State Department officials preparing his book, *The United States in World Affairs, 1945–1947*, written in 1947, wrote that Britain and the United States thought Yugoslavia might have been considering a quick move against Trieste at the time.

million credit previously extended to Czechoslovakia to buy surplus war goods, and to ask the Export-Import Bank to suspend negotiations for another $50 million loan.

This emotional decision was not to America's credit. Apparently, though, this incident did not poison U.S. relations with Czechoslovakia. When the American ambassador to Prague, Laurence A. Steinhardt, returned home at the end of January 1947, he told the press that "there is definitely no iron curtain in Czechoslovakia."

Hungary was able to hold a free election in November 1945, which resulted in an overwhelming victory for the Smallholders Party, an embarrassingly obvious repudiation of the Communists. Thus encouraged, Hungarian politicians hoped they would be able to govern freely. But the Soviet Union prevented any meaningful reorganization of Hungarian society by removing most of the country's assets to Russia as reparations. The United States protested twice to Moscow that the Hungarian economy was being destroyed, but both protests were rejected. The United States also made modest efforts to encourage Hungarian independence from Moscow by giving financial aid.

But Hungary was too vulnerable and too important to the Soviet Union. By late January, a correspondent of *The New York Times* could write from Budapest that "the establishment of a virtual Communist dictatorship is a matter of only weeks. . . ." (In fact, it took nine months.)

The situation continued to deteriorate; in early March, the United States proposed to Britain and the Soviet Union that the Big Three investigate the "outrageous" situation in Hungary, which it ascribed largely to Russia's "unjustified interference" in Hungary's internal affairs. The U.S.S.R. rejected the suggestion and the accusations accompanying it.

The experiences Britain and America shared in Eastern Europe, Germany, at the United Nations and the peace conferences impressed both nations. In each case, the Soviet Union was on one side, Britain and America on the other. The alignment recurred too regularly to be explained as a coincidence. Both Britain and the United States believed they were only pursuing reasonable objectives; neither felt it was trying to encourage bad relations with the Russians. Another explanation was required.

CHAPTER IV

"I doubt very much whether we
have a foreign policy."
—Sir Orme Sargent, *Permanent
Undersecretary of the British
Foreign Office, October 1946.*

T
he first two years after World War II were among the
most hectic in all international history. In earlier eras,
Britain's diplomats might have thrived in such conditions,
but not in 1946. They were no longer the most important
diplomats in the world. Britain was quite suddenly less powerful
and less confident than it had been in almost 150 years. Instead of
guiding events, Britain was guided by them. As a member of the
Attlee government put it several years later, "In relation to the
task before us [after the war], our resources were surely smaller
than those of almost any country."*

As a partner in the alliance that had won the war, Britain had to
assume the victor's responsibilities for the defeated. Britain was
also the protector of an immense though shrinking empire, a role
which brought grave crises in India, Palestine and Greece during
1945–47. Coping with so much would have been difficult in the
best of times, and in many ways, the years immediately after the
war were the worst of times. The old imperial robe no longer fit,
but the British did not know how to replace it.

In 1946 and 1947 Britain was completing the important steps in

* The remark was made by Christopher Mayhew, parliamentary undersecretary in the
Foreign Office from 1946 to 1950, in a speech delivered in June 1950.

its transition from a leading world power to just another European country—though it took years for most of the world to recognize this change, and decades for the British to accept it.

The politicians and diplomats administering British foreign policy after the war did not perceive their own activity in this light. On the contrary, they hoped and intended to salvage British influence, once the country's economy revived. But they didn't have a plan for doing this—so Sir Orme Sargent could doubt whether Britain had a foreign policy.*

While they waited for a new world order to evolve, British officials could pursue specific policies in specific situations which, they were confident, would serve British interests in any eventuality. Such policies were adopted in Germany, Eastern Europe and the United Nations. It was also possible to deal with India and, not quite so easily, Palestine, countries for which Britain had unique responsibility and obvious obligations. In each of these cases, events were too pressing to ignore. But dealing with grave crises one at a time, as they happened to appear, was not a substitute for a foreign policy. The basic question remained: How should Britain stand in relation to the nations of Europe, the empire and the rest of the world?

The question went unanswered. A reply would depend as much on the United States and the Soviet Union as it did on Britain itself, and in London in 1946, there was no confidence in the policies of either of those nations. There are few records of the tactics considered by the British government during that year, but one which has been recorded is most revealing. In March 1946 Attlee suggested to his aides the possibility that Britain withdraw completely from the Middle East, establish a new line of defense across sub-Sahara Africa from Lagos to Nairobi, and station a large body of troops in East Africa. His idea was to minimize the chance of confrontation with the Soviet Union by leaving a wide swath of Arabs and desert between British and Soviet armed forces.

---

* Sir Orme made this observation to Christopher Mayhew in October 1946, when Mayhew asked him for a concise statement of British foreign policy.

Apparently the suggestion was not dismissed out of hand. At least one of Attlee's senior ministers, Hugh Dalton, the Chancellor of the Exchequer, thought it "a fresh and interesting approach." But as a solution to the fundamental problem it had glaring weaknesses. Where would Britain get oil if the Middle East was dominated by a hostile power? How useful would Arabs and desert be if most of Europe was under Russian influence? The more British officials contemplated such "easy" solutions to their dilemma, the more they must have realized how little real control they had over Britain's future position in the world, and how much it would depend on decisions taken in Moscow and Washington.

The alliance with America had been the heart of Britain's war strategy. Early in the war, Churchill had decided that without American participation, victory was doubtful at best. After the United States did declare war, Churchill followed Roosevelt's lead whenever he was unable to persuade F.D.R. to his view, because he thought that nothing was more important than pleasing America. He also believed that the two countries were unlikely to disagree very fundamentally about anything. After the war ended this spirit disappeared.

Roosevelt and Churchill had been close personal friends. But before the war was over, both men were gone from positions of leadership. Their successors shared none of their intimacy and little of their self-confidence in world affairs. In London, Britain's interest in 1946 did not appear so closely identified with America's. The fact that they were fighting the same enemy was enough to hold the two countries together in war, but when the fighting ended, the sense of common purpose diminished. Britain was aware that the same reaction occurred in the United States. America largely forgot its traditional suspicion of Britain during the war, but it returned soon afterward.

Relations with America were much discussed in 1946. Churchill proposed a strong Anglo-American alliance against Communism in his famous speech at Fulton, Missouri, in March. At the time he was widely criticized in Britain, especially by those who feared that Britain and America would "gang up" against the Soviet Union, destroying whatever chance existed for good relations among the Big Three. "We are not ganging up with anybody, neither with one side nor the other," Bevin told the House of Commons emphatically in October 1946.

In the same speech, the Foreign Secretary reminded Parliament that "formerly, it has been said that the role of the United States was to play the part of an intermediary between Britain and Russia. Now," said Bevin, "I see in some of the press, it is suggested that we should play the part of an intermediary between the United States and Russia. Our role is not to be an intermediary at all." Churchill spoke in the same debate a day later: "What I said at Fulton has been outpaced and overpassed by [the] movement of events, and by the movement of American opinion. If I were to make that speech at the present time and in the same place, it would attract no particular attention."

Churchill was exaggerating, but the situation certainly had changed since his speech at Fulton. In August 1946, British and American army officers meeting in Washington began discussing means of cooperation in case of an emergency in Europe. These talks were prompted by the tension in Yugoslavia and by a threatening note from the Soviet Union regarding the Bosphorus and Dardanelles Straits in Turkey. Field Marshal Montgomery visited Washington in September, and told Truman he would like to begin Anglo-American staff consultations that would "cover the whole field of cooperation and combined action in the event of war."

By mentioning the subject to Truman, Montgomery was disobeying instructions from London to "confine my talks to the American Chiefs of Staff," as he later recorded. His instructions reflected the uncertainty in London about America's attitude.

When he arrived in Washington, Montgomery found no ground for such uncertainty. Instead he perceived a "spirit of enthusiastic realism." When he asked Truman about initiating staff talks, the president said, "That's O.K. with me, go right ahead." But Truman and the other American officials who encouraged Montgomery were not interested in an anti-Soviet alliance with Britain. These staff talks and other limited military cooperation* did not amount to any new American commitment to Britain or to Europe.

During late 1946 and early 1947, the British government became gradually more certain of the need for active American participation in European affairs. (British diplomats then in Washington thought that it was one of their most important tasks to encourage the United States to play a bigger role in Europe.) But many Britons doubted that America would ever come to their aid to the extent required. Richard Crossman, a leader of the left wing in the Labour party, expressed an opinion held by more people than his colleagues on the left when he wrote in late January 1947, that collective security would only be possible in Europe if the United States paid for it. "And there is no evidence that any American political leader is even considering such an idea," he wrote.

The doubts of Crossman and others were not groundless. By August 1946 Britain had already clashed twice with the United States on important issues, and on both occasions the American position prevailed at Britain's expense. The subjects at issue were atomic energy and money.

When the war ended, Britain expected to begin an atomic energy program based on the information developed by the British and American scientists who built the atomic bomb. Roosevelt and Churchill had agreed in 1944 that "full collaboration" for "military and commercial [atomic] purposes should

---

* Britain, Canada and the United States agreed to standardize some weapons after the war, largely because of the problems caused by their failure to do so before it began. The U.S. Air Force continued the wartime practice of joint development of some tactics, staff methods and equipment with the R.A.F., and the two air forces exchanged pilots for training at the end of 1946. But there was no integration of British and American commands at any level. The demobilization programs of both countries were continuing apace, and neither was certain what a postwar army would be used for.

continue after the defeat of Japan unless and until terminated by joint agreement." But the spirit of this arrangement—known as the Hyde Park Agreement—died with Roosevelt. Two months after his death officials in Washington could not even find the American copy of the agreement.*

In November 1945 Attlee and Mackenzie King, the Canadian prime minister, came to Washington for talks on atomic energy. These meetings were devoted almost entirely to the problems of securing international control over atomic energy. Anglo-American collaboration was briefly mentioned and left to the Combined Policy Committee composed of representatives of the two governments to sort out.

The Policy Committee drafted an agreement, but it soon emerged that the United States was unwilling to allow a really complete exchange of information. General Leslie Groves, who had headed the Manhattan Project and was secretary of the Policy Committee, expressed the fear that "full collaboration" could amount to an Anglo-American military alliance, and that would be contrary to Article 102 of the United Nations Charter, which required registration and publication of all international agreements. In April 1946 the committee informed Attlee, King and Truman that it had reached a complete impasse.

Attlee cabled a strong protest, reminding Truman that they had agreed to "full and effective" cooperation at the November meeting. He thought the November agreement made it obvious that there would be a complete and free exchange of information, and if the Policy Committee could not find a way to make such an exchange possible, he, Truman and King should find one themselves. Truman answered that the language of the November agreement was "very general." He said that he had never interpreted the agreement to mean that the United States was

---

* It had been filed under "Naval Supplies" by Roosevelt's naval aide, who was confused by the British code name for the atomic project—"Tube Alloys." The American copy was found three years later.

obligated "to furnish the engineering and operation assistance necessary for the construction of another atomic energy plant. Had that been done I would not have signed the memorandum [approved by the three leaders in November]."

Attlee answered at great length. He complained that Britain's contribution to the atomic project was not being fairly rewarded, and that the United States was evading its commitment to help Britain establish its own atomic project.

Truman did not reply immediately because Congress was then considering the McMahon Act, which was passed in late July and signed by the president on August 1, 1946. One of its provisions was that the United States could not share atomic secrets with any other nation. The law naturally displeased official London. Roger Makins, the British diplomat in Washington who was most concerned with atomic problems at the time, has since said, "Congress didn't understand atomic energy. They thought it was an American secret which could be kept. We knew it couldn't be." Britain had lost the opportunity to become an atomic power with American aid, apparently because of domestic American politics. After the McMahon Act became law, Anglo-American atomic cooperation continued only in the field of raw materials.

Peace also complicated financial relations between the United States and Britain. Both countries tentatively decided during the war that postwar prosperity would be best served by liberalizing international trade. Cordell Hull, America's wartime secretary of state, promoted liberal trade as one of the world's most urgent needs. Britain accepted the principle, though not always enthusiastically. Britain knew that the great days of British trade would not return quickly after the war.

Before 1939 Britain had financed a large trade deficit with immense earnings from foreign investment and such "invisibles" as shipping and insurance. Britain would have to export more after the war than it ever had before, and would therefore benefit from lower trade barriers in other countries. This was true as long as no major trading nation suffered a serious depression. Without protection of tariffs and exchange controls, another country's economic problems could quickly become Britain's too.

Many in Britain who feared such a development expected a postwar depression in the United States. The British government's adherence to the idea of liberal trade weakened after the war, when the seriousness of the country's financial situation became obvious. John Maynard Keynes, the government's principal advisor on these matters, concluded that the successful transition to peacetime would have to be financed by aid from outside—obviously, from the United States. For some time, Britain would have to import much more than it could possibly export, to rebuild a strong economy.

This idea was sabotaged by President Truman's premature (and, even he later admitted, ill-advised) decision to terminate lend-lease aid just seven days after Japan surrendered. Keynes had assumed that lend-lease or something like it would finance the transition to peace. Less than a month after lend-lease was cancelled, a British delegation which included Keynes was in Washington in search of aid—preferably a grant, but a loan if a grant was impossible. After three months of difficult negotiations, the United States agreed to a loan of $3.75 billion, plus $650 million to help Britain to pay for lend-lease and purchases of American surplus property. The terms of the loan were not generous. Annual interest of two percent would be charged on the unpaid balance. Britain would have to make sterling freely convertible a year after the agreement went into effect, and meet other stipulations.

Keynes's first request had been for a gift of $6 billion. It was rejected out of hand by the American negotiators, whose principal worry was U.S. public opinion. According to a poll taken in October, 60 percent of the American public opposed the loan; only 20 percent favored it. Influenced by Keynes's difficulties in Washington, the British Cabinet wavered late in November. A number of ministers thought the interest rate and the conditions tied to the loan were unfair. The Cabinet considered recalling Lord Keynes, but he was ill. Sir Edward Bridges, the Permanent Undersecretary of the Treasury, was sent to Washington to see if the United States would not improve its terms. He found the Americans adamant.

On December 6 the Cabinet approved the loan, acting more out of necessity than enthusiasm. Dalton wrote in his diary at the time that "even within the next year or two, circumstances may require a large revision which might even be unilateral." The loan was quickly accepted by the House of Commons, 343–100, although 169 M.P.'s abstained. There was vociferous and articulate opposition on the grounds that the government had accepted too many conditions.

Britain's difficulties with the United States affected public opinion in 1946. According to a Gallup Poll taken in July, 32 percent of the British people felt "less friendly than a year ago" towards the United States. Reports from America may have contributed to this sentiment. For example, a group of schoolboys from Stowe, recording their observations of a trip to America in *The* (London) *Times,* wrote in October: "It is essential to realize how widespread the anti-British feeling in the United States is today."

The left wing of the Labour party exacerbated anti-Americanism by loudly protesting against Britain's apparently close relations with the United States. The left wing had an exaggerated fear of America's proselytizing captains of industry. It freely predicted a collision between American capitalism and the Soviet Union. The left wanted Britain to remain independent and aloof. These anxieties were shared at least momentarily by a much larger section of British opinion after the congressional elections in November. The Republicans' victory was interpreted in much of the British press as a reactionary step backward toward isolationism.

The American Embassy in London reported to Washington in late November that there was "growing uncertainty in Britain of the dependability of [the] U.S. in foreign affairs."° Besides the fear of either American capitalism or U.S. foreign policy, many leaders of British commerce and politics resented the loss of their international preeminence to the United States. And others in all walks of life thought America had failed to recognize or adequately compensate Britain's "disproportionate effort" during the war.

Had Britain been stronger than she was in 1946, the uncertainty of relations with America could have been less important. But the Foreign Office was in no position to pursue an active and independent foreign policy in many parts of the world at once. For the first time in modern history, British diplomacy was restricted by a parsimonious stipend from the Treasury. Foreign policy became the poor brother of domestic policy, itself severely curtailed by a weak economy.

Bevin was especially aware of the disadvantages poverty imposed on diplomacy, and bemoaned his predicament often in the Foreign Office. In a speech in February 1947, he complained: "If I had forty million tons of coal now, I should be three times as powerful in Europe as I am." Yet Bevin knew that one of his principal obligations was to reduce the financial burden of diplomacy on the Exchequer. In mid-August, he wrote Attlee from the Paris Peace Conference: "I am not making the headway I would like in making it possible to reduce our commitments so as to help Hugh [Dalton, the Chancellor]; the Russians are very difficult."

Dalton himself often reminded Bevin of the cost of Britain's international commitments, which the chancellor seemed sometimes to want to eliminate altogether. He struggled against a never-ending stream of commitments and proposals. "I am resisting suggestions from the Foreign Office to spend large sums on Greeks, Turks and Afghans," Dalton wrote in a typical diary entry in November 1946. "I sent a minute to the P.M. saying that we have not got the money for this sort of thing and that, even if we had, we should not spend it on *these* people."

° The words were James Forrestal's, from his diary.

The government could at least afford to make its general policy known on matters which were unlikely to cost Britain any money. Attlee outlined such a general policy in one of his rare statements on foreign affairs to the House of Commons in October 1946. Attlee told the House:

> We believe that men and women must be free, both from the excessive domination of governments, and from the abuses of economic power. We do not seek to thrust our views upon other nations. We are seeking to set an example here of how individual freedom and the interests of the community can be harmonized, and, in our international relations, to afford to all peoples the greatest possible freedom to work out their salvation, consistent with the overriding interests of all in the preservation of peace

These words committed Attlee to nothing at all, but in fairness, he could go no further. The principles Attlee defended were the basis of British foreign policy after the war, though it was sometimes impossible to adhere to them.

Despite the country's economic troubles, the Labour government did not intend to relinquish Britain's status as one of the world's most important nations. The day before Attlee made his general statement in Parliament, Bevin had insisted that Britain "cannot and will not be dismissed." The foreign secretary saw an important role for Great Britain:

> ... Her [Britain's] moral example, her steadiness, and, if I may say so, the economic stability she is now showing after the terrible devastation of war from which she has suffered, place her in a position to render great assistance in the resettlement of the world. We shall stand firm in our purpose; I am sure that the world recognizes the work we are doing, and that, in spite of our difficulties, our prestige and moral leadership are bearing fruit.

Bevin knew, undoubtedly, that "prestige and moral leadership" could bear less fruit than a strong economy might have done. Nevertheless, he would use whatever he had to its best advantage.

Attlee and Bevin both believed that Britain had to remain an important power.

Britain's armed forces shrank rapidly during 1946. From the end of the war to the end of 1946, 4.9 million men and women were demobilized from British forces, leaving a total defense establishment of about 1.5 million. But the government made it clear that this process would not continue indefinitely. In November 1946 Attlee announced that conscription would continue during peacetime. "That decision meant that Britain was prepared to accept all its responsibilities," one Cabinet member has said.

Attlee was strongly criticized inside the Labour party, primarily by the left wing, for maintaining conscription, but there is no indication that he hesitated to do so. The British people approved the decision, though not overwhelmingly. In March 1946, 55 percent of those polled by the Gallup organization supported "compulsory military service for men in peacetime." Conscription was a symbol, and a relatively inexpensive one, of Britain's intention to maintain its international position.

The Labour government's dedication to the United Nations was similarly symbolic. The idea of the United Nations was enthusiastically supported in the Labour party, for it coincided with Labour's own international policies. For Attlee and Bevin, who were less inclined than many of their colleagues in the party to regard international affairs philosophically, the organization had obvious practical advantages. If it operated properly, the United Nations could be the stabilizing force Britain felt the world needed so badly, but could not provide itself.

Hector McNeil, Bevin's senior assistant as Minister of State in the Foreign Office, emphasized this point in October 1946. McNeil said that the "basis of our foreign policy must rest upon the United Nations, and the instruments of the United Nations must be upheld." Only the United Nations, he said, could satisfy the reasonable demands of the world's nations and thwart the unreasonable ones.

Thus without great resources, without reliable help from the United States, but determined not to abdicate its international authority, Britain coped with the many discouraging problems it faced after the Second World War.

India was Britain's most serious postwar dilemma, and probably the most complicated, too. Since 1942, when the War Cabinet had authorized Sir Stafford Cripps to devise a plan for Indian independence, it had been obvious that Britain would have to relinquish the jewel of the empire. Attlee made self-rule for India a firm policy of his government soon after he took office. But many serious difficulties separated Attlee's declaration of intent from the reality of a self-governing India.

The most serious, as Attlee had known since his service on the Simon Commission in the late 1920s, was the bitter division between Hindus and Moslems. The two religious communities disagreed about virtually everything except the desirability of Indian independence. This was evident in June 1945 when Cripps's plan for independence within the Commonwealth was presented to Moslem and Hindu leaders. Mohammed Ali Jinnah of the Moslem League insisted then that an independent Moslem state, Pakistan, should be cut out of India. By the time Attlee's government was able to begin serious consideration of the Indian problem, the positions of the Moslem League and the Hindu Congress Party were hardening against any compromise.

Attlee sent a cabinet committee to India in March 1946. Its mission was to bring the two sides together, which it did, but only briefly and superficially. Lord Wavell, the British viceroy in India, tried several different solutions to the Moslem-Hindu quarrel, but none worked. In November 1946 Attlee ordered Wavell home for urgent consultations, and asked him to bring Nehru and Jinnah with him. Only after the prime minister intervened personally would Nehru agree to come to London. (Attlee considered him a personal friend.) These talks lasted only four days before Nehru walked out. Throughout December, January and early February, London's efforts to find a compromise were unsuccessful.

On February 20, 1947 (one day before Britain informed the United States that it would cease all aid to Greece and Turkey), Attlee told the House of Commons that his government would withdraw entirely from India not later than June 1948. He would give power to whomever seemed capable of exercising it. He left no doubt that if there was no representative regime of Hindus and Moslems in existence by that time, India would be partitioned along religious lines into two countries.

The decision to leave India was one of the great turning points in British history. But at the time, it was a natural development. The impulse toward self-rule among Asian peoples after the war was intense.* Britain had admitted as much in 1942, when even Churchill had to agree to give Cripps the authority to promise the Indians independence when the war was over.

The British public certainly seemed reconciled to Indian independence. The Labour party was committed to withdrawing from India, and sought only to find a way to do it. By early 1947 the British had no more room for maneuver. As Cripps said when Parliament debated India in early March 1947, Britain had in effect given up control over India by "Indianizing" almost all of the administration. "One thing that was quite clearly impossible was to decide to continue our responsibility indefinitely," Cripps said. A leading Conservative made a similar point in the House of Lords, and did it so forcefully that the peers decided not to vote on Attlee's announcement, a tacit endorsement of the government's decision. The Tory was Lord Halifax, a former viceroy of India, who said the government should only be attacked by those who could offer a realistic alternative to its policies. He could think of none.

Attlee's February 20 announcement was preceded by hectic

---

* In 1946 Indonesia and the Philippines both won their independence, and Ho Chi Minh began his fight against the French to free Vietnam from colonial control. In January 1947 Britain promised Burma its independence "as soon as possible."

efforts to find some better solution than it eventually offered. Attlee, who knew most of the Indian personalities involved and thought he understood India's problems, was active in all these efforts. His friend Francis Williams, an aide in Downing Street at the time, has written that the prime minister "was more directly and personally involved" in Far Eastern problems "than almost any other issue throughout the course of his whole administration." "I handled India," Attlee himself said many years later. In his own mind, the decision on India was probably more important than anything that occurred in late 1946 and early 1947 save the fuel crisis.

Attlee was a calculating politician. The calculations he made about India and its leaders, though not flattering, were sympathetic, and probably correct. Recalling his decision to make the February 20 announcement years afterward, Attlee said:

> I'd come to the conclusion from my own experience of India that there was a great deal of happiness for them in asking for everything, and putting down everything that was wrong in India to British rule, and then sitting pretty. I thought that most of them were not really keen on responsibility. They would talk and talk and talk, and as long as they could put the responsibility on us, they would continue to quarrel among themselves. Therefore I concluded that the thing to do was to bring them right up against it . . . [and] set a time limit. . . .

In mid-January, Dalton wrote in his diary that "India has receded a little from the front of the picture [in the Cabinet]. All our long discussions on a public statement to bring things up to the point by naming a fixed retiring date have for the moment run into the sand."

How long had Attlee favored the idea of setting an arbitrary withdrawal date? Perhaps since early December, when his meetings with Jinnah and Nehru had ended in failure. In any case, the evidence is strong that he was moving deliberately toward a solution of the Indian problem for several months before his

February statement. The decision itself was apparently taken easily. It is not known whether the Cabinet debated the February 20 statement before it was made, or Attlee just informed his colleagues that he planned to make it. Quite possibly it was the second disguised as the first.

Attlee appreciated the possibility of conveying the illusion of power to his Cabinet without always providing the substance. In this case, it is likely that Attlee had the support of Cripps and Pethwick-Lawrence, his two principal experts on India, and in a general sense, he had the avid support of the whole Cabinet and the Labour party for any policy which would quickly lead to Indian self-government.

Much more quietly, Britain's second largest colony in the Far East, Burma, was given its independence at almost the same time. The Burmese were united, and well represented by the Anti-Fascist People's Freedom League, which was eager to lead the country into independence. In December 1946 the British government invited a delegation of Burmese to London on the understanding that they would discuss means of granting independence. After talks lasting almost a month, agreements were published in London which gave the Burmese an interim government at once, and a promise of full independence "within or without the Commonwealth . . . as soon as possible."

Attlee had decided that in India, partition was better than the *status quo*. In Palestine, even partition was apparently impossible, yet the division between the Arabs and Jews was as bitter and profound as that between Moslems and Hindus. Britain was caught between the two.

Britain first occupied Palestine during World War I. More than one British government announced its intention to create a national homeland for Jews in the territory, but this never happened. Palestine was a victim of wartime politics, and of British interest in maintaining Arab goodwill. (The entire Arab world vigorously opposed a Jewish state in Palestine.)

The Labour party came to power as strong proponents of a Jewish state in Palestine. The party's position in the 1945 election campaign was explicit: Jews should be admitted to Palestine "in such numbers as to become a majority." (At war's end the population was 1.2 million Arabs and 550,000 Jews.) But Labour's attitude changed in office. Attlee and Bevin accepted the arguments of the Foreign Office that relations with the Arab world were too important to jeopardize by supporting Zionism. Their change of heart was not well received within the Labour party, especially by a large and vocal pro-Zionist faction of Labour M.P.'s. Government ministers told these rebels privately that there were three reasons why the Palestine policy had been changed: to assuage Arab opinion, to keep the Arab states out of the Soviet sphere of influence, and to save money. Apparently, the Foreign Office was convinced that the Arab states of the Middle East would be easy prey for Soviet propaganda if Britain could be accused of pro-Zionist sympathies. And it would be too expensive to allow more Jews into Palestine because the number of British troops required to keep order rose in direct proportion to the number of Jews in the territory.

Appeasing the Arabs meant angering the United States. One of President Truman's first communications with Attlee after the Potsdam conference was a request that 100,000 immigration permits to Palestine be granted at once to Jewish refugees from Nazism. (Truman had just read an aide's report, which he forwarded to Attlee, on the appalling living conditions of several hundred thousand Jewish refugees in Germany and Austria.) Attlee refused then and on several later occasions to accept Truman's proposal. But Britain realized that America's interest in Palestine was too strong to ignore, and in October 1945 Attlee did agree to a joint Anglo-American commission of inquiry to study the Palestine question. Britain wanted the commission to consider the problems of Jewish refugees generally, and to determine whether countries other than Palestine might accept Jewish immigrants. Truman refused. "I did not want the United States to become party to any dilatory tactics," he later wrote.

In April 1946 this committee recommended that Palestine eventually become an independent state dominated neither by Arabs or Jews, but that until the two groups were ready for such an arrangement, British administration should continue. The committee also thought that 100,000 immigration permits were needed immediately, a recommendation that pleased Truman. But the British reaction was unenthusiastic, and no action was ever taken on the committee's report. Attlee continued to hope that an agreement could be reached which was acceptable to his government and to the United States. He suggested a meeting of British and American experts on Palestine, and Truman agreed. This new committee met in London in July 1946. After just two weeks, the tentative conclusions it had reached were leaked to the press. The committee had decided to recommend that Palestine be divided into Jewish, Arab and British sectors. The Arab and Jewish states would participate in a central government with limited powers, though including the power to control immigration.

Both Jews and Arabs rejected this proposal, and so, eventually, did President Truman. By autumn, as Truman wrote a friend, the Palestine problem seemed "insoluble." And it was made even more difficult by a perceptible hardening of anti-Jewish feeling in Britain which followed a series of terrorist attacks on British personnel in Palestine. The most dramatic incident occurred on July 22, when an explosion at the King David Hotel, Britain's headquarters in Jerusalem, killed almost 100 people. Every subsequent act of terrorism was reported in bitter detail in Britain.

President Truman was not the only important personality who refused to accept the orthodox Foreign Office view of Palestine (which was also shared by his own State Department). Churchill had pro-Zionist tendencies and often criticized the Attlee government's position. "At present," he said in October 1946, "we have no policy [for Palestine], as far as I can make out, nor have we had one for more than a year."

Several members of Attlee's Cabinet also remained unpersuaded by the diplomats' arguments. Shinwell and Aneurin Bevan, the Minister of Health, both supported a Jewish national home in Palestine. But as Bevan explained more than once to an unhappy colleague, "We never get a chance to discuss Palestine in the Cabinet."° It was discussed in small committees of the Cabinet—committees whose members were chosen arbitrarily by the prime minister. But Palestine only rarely came before the full Cabinet, and when it did, Attlee and Bevin were able to control the discussion.

They could not control discussion inside the Labour party, where the Palestine question evoked strong emotions. A group identified with Labour's left wing and led by Richard H.S. Crossman adopted the Jewish cause in Palestine with fervor. They attacked those who had changed party policy most bitterly for abandoning the moral principles on which it had originally been based. "The contrast between the government's handling of the Indian and the Palestine problems could not be more abrupt," wrote Crossman and Michael Foot in one acerbic pamphlet in 1946. (Attlee and Bevin must have realized the effectiveness of this argument, not least in the United States, where Britain's Palestine policy looked like old-fashioned imperialism to many people.)

Crossman and many of his colleagues thought that Bevin and Attlee were both anti-Semites of a kind, who arbitrarily refused to give the Zionists any sympathy. Such accusations were not made without evidence. In June 1946 Bevin complained that Americans supported a home for Jews in Palestine "because they didn't want

---

° The unhappy colleague was R.H.S. Crossman, who recalled Bevan's remark in an interview with the author. In 1946 Crossman found Bevan's disclaimer quite amazing. But in 1966, after he had spent two years as a Cabinet minister himself, Crossman said he understood it completely.

too many of them in New York." Crossman has said that Attlee could not understand why the Jews "refused to stay a religion," and he would never admit that they might indeed be a nation. It is a plausible suggestion; Attlee was, after all, a product of London's East End, where the Jews were very much like everyone else, and suffered from no peculiar nationalism. Even if this explanation is unfair, it is not surprising that a man like Attlee, with a strong English middle-class sense of propriety, reacted as he did to the Palestine dispute, especially after Zionist terrorists began killing British soldiers and civilians.

The government enjoyed substantial public support for its Palestine policy, largely because Zionist terrorism angered ordinary Englishmen. Not that public support was necessary. There is no tradition of democratic foreign policy-making in Britain. Foreign policy has not been an important electoral issue for any political party since 1935, and members of Parliament are seldom responsive to public opinion on subjects which have no bearing on their election. There is no real opportunity for a back-bench M.P., who is usually controlled by party discipline, to influence foreign policy. Even the Cabinet is expected to leave foreign affairs to the prime minister and his foreign secretary, unless invited to discuss them. In modern times, foreign policy was a decisive issue in determining the fate of a government only in 1939, and then the whole matter was resolved neatly within the Conservative party without reference to public opinion.

Suez in 1956 was a similar case. An inflamed public could have only a negative influence on the course of events, and even then popular opinion might have been ignored if the Tories had remained united behind their prime minister. In 1914, Britain declared war by an act of the Privy Council. Only one government minister was present, and he was Lord Beauchamp, not even an elected politician. That was a different era, but the tradition endures that the British people leave foreign affairs to their rulers.

Public opinion in Britain did affect the Zionists, who realized that the British people were increasingly unsympathetic to their cause. The Zionists also understood that many people thought Britain's Palestine policy was based on anti-Semitism in the government. Therefore they saw no good reason to accept the arguments of Ernest Bevin during 1946 and early 1947 and agree to a compromise solution. Why cooperate, the Zionists must have thought, with a man or a nation prejudiced against you, especially when so many other reputable nations and individuals thought your requests were fair?

Nevertheless Bevin continued to try. He negotiated several times that fall and winter with Jewish and Arab delegations. In the midst of one round of talks with the Jews, President Truman repeated his suggestion that 100,000 Jewish refugees be allowed into Palestine at once. The president's statement coincided with Yom Kippur, the Jewish Day of Atonement. Truman advised Attlee that he would make the statement, and Attlee had asked him to postpone it, as Bevin was then negotiating with the Jews and thought he had "found the right approach at last."

Attlee feared Truman's statement might upset those talks. But the president went ahead. He was undoubtedly prompted by the rumor that Governor Thomas Dewey of New York, a leading Republican, was about to propose that several hundred thousand immigration permits be granted. (Dewey made such a suggestion a few days later. Coincidentally, the congressional elections were just a month away.) Bevin, who was in Paris with Byrnes at the time, complained angrily to his American colleague about the president's remark. Byrnes explained the domestic political aspect of the incident, but privately disassociated himself from the president's statement.

Bevin's negotiations with the Jews did fail, but there is no evidence that Truman's statement was responsible. British officials had decided that the Truman administration was unwilling to see Palestine as they did because of short-term American political considerations. One British diplomat visiting Washington that fall began his consultations at the State Department by saying, "We realize you can't do anything until after the

COLD WINTER, COLD WAR

elections, but—" He was interrupted, and reminded that there was an election every two years. The British Government never realized how appealing the Zionist cause was to Americans, for whom Arabs were only characters riding camels in movies, and who thought the war had been fought in part to help the Jews of Europe.

Bevin made his last effort to solve the crisis in January, when he summoned Arab and Jewish representatives to London. The principal Jewish leaders had lost faith in Bevin and were reluctant to accept his invitation. Many of them eventually refused it. Those who came soon rejected the British proposals for a partitioned state ruled by a central government, based on the suggestions of the second Anglo-American committee. According to press reports at the time, even then the British negotiators were not certain about what they were offering. Arthur Creech Jones, the colonial secretary, was said to have told the Jews at one point that they would have the right to secede from the central government after five years if it was unworkable. "No," Bevin reportedly interrupted, "not the right to secede."

The story may have been an exaggeration, but it was a credible exaggeration. Bevin's health was bad at the time (he suffered a mild heart attack six weeks later), and his patience with Jews and Arabs was exhausted. The Arabs were no more amenable than the Jews to his exhortations. Bevin gave up and ended talks on February 12, 1947—nine days before Britain told America of its plan to cut off aid to Greece and Turkey. Two days later, at Bevin's suggestion, the Cabinet voted to refer the Palestine problem to the United Nations.

Bevin did not regard this as the end of the struggle. He expected the United Nations to send the problem back from whence it came after discovering how difficult it was to find a solution that pleased both Arabs and Jews.° But it was a defeat, and a painful one.

"Bevin thought he could be the great savior of the Middle

° In the event the United Nations did solve the problem by creating the State of Israel, Bevin had no further involvement in Palestine.

East," Shinwell has recalled. Events proved he was not. Announcing the Cabinet's decision to refer Palestine to the United Nations, Bevin predicted that "in the end, the problem of Jews and Arabs can be settled. After 2000 years of conflict, twelve months will not be a long delay." A week later, when Parliament debated Palestine, Bevin was even more caustic. He recounted the incident of Truman's Yom Kippur statement about 100,000 immigration permits, and Byrnes's explanation of the domestic political factors involved, and complained: "In international affairs, I cannot settle things if my problem is made the subject of local elections. I hope I am not saying anything to cause bad feeling with the United States, but I feel so intensely about this."

These were the words of a man who had let himself get too personally involved in a diplomatic dispute, a dispute he had little right to call "my problem." Not surprisingly, Bevin's speech did cause bad feeling in the United States. Truman was infuriated, but held his temper. He issued a statement denying any political motivation for his Yom Kippur remarks, and his press secretary let it be known that the president regarded Bevin's speech as a personal affront. But the incident went no further. The next day, Bevin insisted that the Palestine disagreement "stands by itself. On all other questions," Bevin said, "our relations with the United States are of the most cordial character." He was essentially correct. The ill-feeling between London and Washington regarding Palestine did not seem to affect any other aspect of Anglo-American relations.

While struggling with the problems of one of the smallest and weakest territories in the Middle East, Britain was also having trouble with one of the biggest and wealthiest, Egypt. The Egyptians resented the use of their country as a battlefield in World War II. When the war ended, anti-British feeling in Egypt grew bitter. The Egyptian government pressed Britain for a revision of the 1936 treaty which allowed British troops into Egypt. Moderate British proposals for rewriting the treaty, including the withdrawal of all British troops, did not satisfy increasingly militant Egyptian politicians, who in late 1946 began to insist that the Sudan be ceded to the Egyptian crown as part of any new settlement. By the end of January 1947, the two countries were further than ever from agreement, and Egypt broke off negotiations. It was not a grave problem, nor an especially pressing one, but Egypt did provide another unwanted diversion for Britain's harried diplomats in 1946–47. This was another reminder of how difficult it was for Britain to balance its various interests in the postwar world.

Britain became involved in Greek affairs in October 1944, after German forces had withdrawn and a small contingent of British troops landed in Greece to occupy the country. It was a quiet beginning to two-and-a-half years of expensive frustrations.

Greece was devastated by the war. Continual disinvestment of resources had reduced most of the population to a subsistence existence. Yet Britain had neither sufficient resources nor enthusiasm for a massive aid program. Britain's interest in the country was strategic. Churchill had agreed with Stalin in October 1944 that Britain would have an ascendant position in Greece, and that the Russians would be dominant in Rumania and Bulgaria. But the strategic advantage of keeping Greece outside the Soviet orbit was not cheaply bought. Between 1944 and March 1947, Greece cost the Exchequer £87 million ($348 million) in direct expenditures, and more in contributions to the United Nations Relief and Rehabilitation Administration.

Soon after the first British troops arrived, they were fighting with one faction of Greeks against another. In December 1944 the combined force of the National Liberation Front and National Popular Liberation Army provoked a virtual civil war, and only because of British assistance were the non-Communist, progovernment forces able to prevail. Two months later, their army badly defeated, the Communists agreed to a truce. The British troops had prevented Communist domination of Greece by force, but their participation in what seemed to be an internal Greek struggle was suspect.

Early in 1946 the Soviet Union charged that the continued presence of British troops in Greece was a threat to peace. In early February the Security Council of the United Nations debated this Soviet accusation. The debate was acrimonious and unproductive. Bevin surprised many observers with his harsh words. He said that Britain's presence in Greece was no threat to peace, but there was a real threat—"the incessant propaganda from Moscow and the utilization of the Communist parties in every country in the world as a means to attack the British people and the British government." The council was meeting in London, and its deliberations had maximum exposure in the British press. Many members of the Labour party were appalled at Bevin's outspoken attack on the Russians. They felt Bevin had adopted a Churchillian policy in Greece to maintain a corrupt, right-wing government regardless of the popular will.

British politicians who favored withdrawal from Greece had two appealing arguments. One was moralistic—that Britain was supporting the wrong faction in Greece for the wrong reasons (the argument many of the same people made in regard to Palestine). The second was painfully practical—that with all its economic problems at home, Britain could not afford to maintain the dilapidated Greek economy, which was a bottomless receptacle for British aid. The first point was debatable, but the second was not, and the British government never hid its desire to withdraw from Greece as soon as possible.

The critics' first argument was weakened in March when an apparently fair parliamentary election was held in Greece, and conservative, pro-royalist candidates won a large majority. But the Communists boycotted this election, and attacked its results as meaningless. In April a slightly more broadly based government under Constantine Tsaldaris took office. In the following months, Bevin and Byrnes often suggested to Tsaldaris that he appease his government's critics (the most vocal of whom, outside the Soviet orbit, were in Britain and America) by distributing ministerial portfolios among the politicians of most of Greece's political parties. Tsaldaris made only small efforts to comply with these suggestions during the nine months he was prime minister.

Britain was reluctant to hold a plebiscite on the future of the monarchy, fearing that the turmoil in Greece precluded a meaningful referendum. This was a particularly sensitive problem, because to the left-wing critics of British policy, the monarchy had become a symbol of corrupt conservatism. But the conservative, pro-royalist elements which won the March elections were eager to hold the plebiscite as soon as possible, and when the first Greek parliament in ten years opened in May, it scheduled the plebiscite for September 1, 1946. The British acquiesced. All parties, including the Communists, decided to participate, and the voting was entirely fair in the eyes of American, British and French observers. The result was quite remarkable; 69 percent of 1.6 million voters supported the king's return.

By September 1946 the British Cabinet had obviously decided that it had to reduce Britain's commitments in Greece. Evidently, Bevin and those who defended a strong British role had lost the initiative to Dalton and others who had decided that Greece was more than Britain could afford. No abrupt decision was made during the summer, but British policy was changing. When Tsaldaris came to London in July for a series of discussions with British ministers, most of his many requests were set aside for further consideration. During these talks, Dalton told Tsaldaris: "We must bring in the Americans; alone we cannot bear this burden [of aid to Greece]." The Greek premier had to return to Athens with little to show for a long visit. Apparently Britain had not even promised to continue support for the Greek army through the end of Greece's fiscal year (March 31, 1947), though Tsaldaris received this assurance soon afterward.

Sometime during August or early September, Byrnes and Bevin had a talk about Greece in Paris. Byrnes agreed that the United

States would assume some responsibility for aiding Greece—how much is not certain. He apparently indicated that America would be willing to provide economic aid, and hoped Britain would continue to support the Greek military establishment.

Did the British take this as an assurance that the United States would step into Greece if they had to step out? At that time, it is doubtful whether Bevin really expected Britain to be forced to withdraw almost completely. He was one of the British Cabinet ministers who was convinced that Britain's economic troubles were essentially financial, and would be overcome once a favorable balance of trade was restored. There is no record that he ever thought Britain's successive concessions to economic necessity amounted to an abdication of its international position.

Bevin's place in history is assured by his identification with the smooth change from the *Pax Britannica* to the *Pax Americana,* but he probably would have denied that any such thing occurred while he was foreign secretary. He seemed to believe that American dollars could sustain Britain's status as a major power, and sustain it without serious complications.

In any case, Byrnes's accommodating words were certainly reassuring. They must have made it easier for the British Cabinet to decide to go ahead with the withdrawal of more than 15,000 troops from Greece during September and October. This was about half the number of British soldiers then in Greece; their withdrawal, according to the government, was part of a general redeployment of forces necessitated by the continuing demobilization of wartime armies. At the time the withdrawal did not seem to be part of a general British retreat from Greece.

In October Bevin told the House of Commons that Britain still had commitments there—that Greece still needed British aid to "develop, in her own way and without interference, her democratic institutions," and to improve economic conditions.

Troops were another matter. Answering a question from Churchill, Bevin said in the same debate, "we shall get them out as soon as . . . certain obligations . . . are fulfilled." It seems fair to wonder whether Bevin really knew what Britain would do in the months ahead. The Greek situation, like most sources of international tension in 1946–47, was too unstable to be predictable.

During the last months of 1946, American interest in the Mediterranean area increased. This was welcome news in London (where, it will be recalled, only months before, Attlee had suggested withdrawal to southern Africa as a solution to Britain's problems in the Near East). Britain took advantage of America's new interest. Until the summer of 1946, when the American Congress approved the British loan, the Greek government felt that Britain opposed a direct Greek approach to the United States for aid. Even as late as mid-November, the British mission in Athens discouraged a Greek suggestion that military aid be solicited from America. But a few days later Britain allowed Greece to ask the United States for military assistance. No doubt, American aid looked increasingly attractive to both Greece and Britain as the Greek guerrillas advanced and the Greek and British economies retreated.

On January 13, 1947, Bevin told the Greek ambassador in London to address further requests for aid to Washington. Presumably, this was a temporary instruction. Bevin, like the United States at this time, was stalling. Later in January, Britain made plans to withdraw more troops from Greece, though when news of this leaked (or was leaked) to the press, a Foreign Office spokesman insisted that it did "not imply a British withdrawal." On January 31, the Foreign Office told the American chargé d'affaires in London that the Cabinet had just "agreed in principle that Great Britain should lend further assistance to Greece."

British policy looks confused and contradictory in retrospect, and it probably was at the time. The Greek problem was an immense one, but it could be put off and postponed and temporarily forgotten more easily than India or Palestine or several other crises of those months. But when the diplomats set it aside, the economists in the Treasury seized the initiative. The commitment to Greece was curtailed for economic reasons throughout late 1946 and early 1947 while the political implications of the Greek crisis were temporarily ignored. Like so many postwar problems, this one could not really be left alone at all; if decisions were not made, events would soon dictate them.

India, Palestine and Greece were all problems which required British action, and they were therefore more distracting than disputes at the United Nations, for instance, or even than the quest for peace treaties. But one problem which required no immediate action was at least as distracting as those that did—the question of Britain's policy toward Europe and, above all, the Soviet Union.

In 1946 Europe was exhausted and largely in ruins. The giants of the continent, Germany, France and Italy, were impotent, and the future of Europe could only be a subject for speculation. Bevin never revealed any great expectations for European recovery or future European importance. Soon after taking office, the Attlee government apparently rejected as unrealistic the suggestion that Europe should become a third force—a "balance" between Russia and America. Nevertheless, Bevin and Attlee both hoped that significant European cooperation would be possible.

That desire had one tangible result in 1946–47—a new treaty of alliance with France against Germany. The treaty, originally conceived by Leon Blum, was agreed to in January 1947, and signed in March. But cooperation was difficult even with France, the only nation in Europe (other than Germany) strong enough to be taken seriously by Britain in 1946. Bevin once recalled telling Georges Bidault, the French foreign minister, in 1946, that "we can't carry on a conversation between two Great Powers with a third Great Power in the cupboard with a listening apparatus." At that time, the Communists in the French government had insisted that the traditional *chef du cabinet* in each ministry be replaced by three men, one of them always a Communist.

The "third Great Power in the cupboard," of course, was the Soviet Union. Britain never regarded Russia as an intimate ally. There was none of the rapport between the two of the kind which made relations easy, for instance, between Britain and France, or Britain and the United States. Churchill had disguised Britain's many differences with Russia in 1941, when he unreservedly welcomed Stalin's help against the Nazis. In fact, Churchill himself never sought and never expected a fundamental rapprochement between Britain and the Soviet Union.

By all indications, Britain's professional diplomats were also pessimistic. But while Churchill was prime minister, the Russians were never treated with contempt or hostility. Churchill tried to find the basis for a workable postwar relationship by persuading Stalin to divide some of the contested areas of Europe, in effect, into spheres of British and Soviet influence. That was in October 1944. Stalin agreed then to Churchill's proposals for the Balkans and Hungary, but he soon began to disregard his agreement.

Many members of the Labour party regarded the Soviet Union as a congenial friend. They were not Communists, but confirmed Socialists so eager to praise Soviet socialism that they were able to see only what they approved, and ignore what might not have pleased them. Labour M.P.'s who were less ready to profess open friendship were nevertheless convinced that the Tories had mishandled the Bolsheviks since 1922, and that a Labour government could do much better. Labour's manifesto for the 1945 general election expressed such sentiments: "... Let it not be forgotten that in the years leading up to the war the Tories were so scared of Russia that they missed the chance to establish a partnership which might well have prevented the war." The same document reminded the electorate of "Labour's one great asset: it has a common bond with the working peoples of all countries. . . ."

"Left will be able to speak to left," Bevin promised the party conference in June 1945, although Attlee said later he never believed that was true. But foreign affairs were barely mentioned by the party in the 1945 campaign; only one page in twelve of the manifesto (the British equivalent of a party platform) was devoted to international problems, and it to the kind of generalizations already mentioned. They had little effect on Attlee's government. If Bevin really thought Stalin would be friendlier to a Labour government than he had been to Churchill, his experience at Potsdam immediately after taking office must have changed his mind. Stalin, it turned out, held a traditional Bolshevik animosity for Social Democrats like Attlee and Bevin, and in fact seemed to find them less congenial than he did Churchill and Anthony Eden. During the first year after the war, Soviet anti-British propaganda was much more common than anti-American propaganda. During that year, left fell out with left.

Bevin's blunt complaint in the February 1946 Security Council debate on Greece about "incessant propaganda from Moscow" revealed his own disillusionment. Two months after that outburst, the British government announced it would begin Russian-language radio broadcasts to Russia, a decision generally interpreted as a reply to Soviet propaganda.

Relations did not improve during the spring and summer, but Bevin declined to make any final decisions about the Soviet Union. His own attitude remained firm. Twice during August 1946 he approved strong rebukes against what appeared to be attempted Russian incursions into the Middle East.* On the basis of these developments and, more obviously, the unfriendly tone of the Paris Peace Conference, Reuters' diplomatic correspondent wrote in late August that relations among the Big Three had "reached a new low level."

Bevin told a colleague in early September that he could not understand the Russians' intransigence. He found Molotov "like a communist in a local Labour party. If you treated him badly, he only made the most of the grievance and, if you treated him well, he only put his price up and abused you the next day." Bevin tried

---

* The first of these occasions was a Foreign Office statement issued August 9 warning that any "violent or sudden" threat to British interests in Iran would be met with immediate action—so immediate that "there may not be time to consult the United Nations." The second was Bevin's personal endorsement of a firm U.S. rejection of the Russian suggestion that the Turkish straits be administered jointly by the Black Sea powers, including the Soviet Union.

to engage the Russians by suggesting an extension of the Anglo-Soviet mutual assistance treaty of 1942 for twenty or even fifty years, but the Russians ignored this proposal throughout the fall. During a debate on foreign affairs in the House of Commons in October 1946, Bevin admitted that at the Paris Peace Conference, "there have appeared to be two *blocs* when we came to the voting." But the foreign secretary remained hopeful: "Such divisions must, and I am sure can, be prevented."

In the same debate, Bevin's deputy, Hector McNeil, made a much more revealing speech. Churchill had just challenged the government to answer one question: "Is it or is it not true that there are today more than 200 Soviet divisions on a war footing in the occupied territories of Europe from the Baltic to Vienna, and from Vienna to the Black Sea?" McNeil said that he must reply "in measured terms." He was unable to say how many Russian troops were in Eastern Europe, and he would not speculate on their possible uses. It was British policy, he said, "to assume that responsible governments meant what they said in public" until there was proof of the contrary. He admitted there was "cause for alarm" in the Russian buildup in Eastern Europe, but he thought perhaps this could be explained:

> There is a historic confusion repeated again and again in the minds of men and in the minds of nations between the conditions of peace and the conditions of national security. It is, perhaps, best expressed in the old cliché that a rifle is a weapon of defense when you look at it from the butt, and a weapon of attack when you look at it from the muzzle. It may also be true, I expect, that our activities and the activities of the United States look to be muzzle-ended from the Soviet point of view.

For Churchill and others who were convinced that good relations with the Soviet Union were impossible, McNeil's was an unsatisfactory speech. But there is no evidence that it was anything but an honest one. In late 1946 the British government believed that the blackest interpretation of Soviet motives was not justified. Yet it was prepared to accept that interpretation if its accuracy became incontrovertible. It cost Britain nothing to assume "that responsible governments meant what they said in public," and, therefore, that Russia did want a fair peace settlement. Britain decided not to antagonize the Soviet Union deliberately, but not to appease it either.

In November Attlee reminded the world of this unwillingness to appease in a firm speech to the Lord Mayor's Banquet. The prime minister criticized those who used the United Nations for propaganda, and said Britain had "exercised the greatest restraint" by not replying to unwarranted abuse. The diplomatic correspondent of the *Glasgow Herald* wrote afterward that the speech was widely regarded in London as "a last warning to the Russians that cooperation is a bilateral business." But there was still optimism in "official circles" that a satisfactory arrangement with the Russians was possible—"perhaps it is the sort of negative optimism which believes that somehow the worst just cannot happen," he wrote.

Many people, including a number of Labour members of Parliament, thought the worst could be prevented, if only the government would adopt a more accommodating policy toward the Soviet Union. This attitude became identified with the group on the left wing informally led by Richard Crossman. Their grumblings were heard, on the "Russian issue" as well as on Palestine and Greece, throughout 1946, but until November they made little trouble. On November 12 a group of M.P.'s tabled an amendment to the Address from the Throne which asked the government to "review and recast" its foreign policy to encourage collaboration with "all nations and groups striving to secure full Socialist planning and control of the world's resources, and thus provide a democratic and constructive Socialist alternative to an otherwise inevitable conflict between American capitalism and Soviet communism. . . ."

Government ministers pleaded with the parliamentary Labour party to remain loyal to Bevin's foreign policy, but without complete success. The amendment eventually attracted fifty-seven signatures, a number seized on by an anonymous muse who dubbed Crossman and his followers the "fifty-seven varieties." Twenty-one of the most extreme left-wing members of this group sent Attlee a "private" letter (its contents were soon revealed by the *Daily Worker*) expounding their views on foreign policy. They criticized the government's preoccupation with Soviet Russia which, they wrote, appeared "most one-sided" in light of the extension of American military bases, America's monopoly of the atomic bomb, "her [America's] inflated military budget and the capitalist expansionist nature of her economy." Many people in Britain and abroad made the mistake of identifying all of the "fifty-seven varieties" with these views.

Parliament debated the amendment to the address on November 18. Crossman opened for the rebels with a careful and articulate speech. He claimed no extreme position for those who had signed the amendment; his fear was that the government was abandoning Labour's cherished stance as a "bridge builder" that could mediate between Russia and America. Attlee himself responded for the government. He described Crossman's amendment as "misconceived, mistimed and based on a misconception of fact." Concerning the Soviet Union, "not very much will be found to distinguish the policy of prerevolutionary Russia and that of postrevolutionary Russia." Bevin's policy, said the prime minister, was the entire government's policy. Was it a socialist policy? "The attacks I have seen made on the foreign secretary," said Attlee, "are made often by people whose services to the cause of labor and Socialism are as dust in the balance compared with his."

At the end of the debate, feeling his point had been made, Crossman asked to withdraw the amendment without a vote. But the Conservatives were eager to embarrass the government, and refused the unanimous consent necessary for such a move. The amendment was voted on and defeated 353-0. But about one hundred Labour M.P.'s deliberately abstained.* It was a high

* There is no official count of abstentions in the House of Commons. The most careful estimates in the press ranged from 94 to 126.

figure, high enough to give the incident a place in the history of Attlee's government as the "stab in the back" motion against Bevin, who was in the United States at the time. (A second amendment to the address, protesting the continuation of conscription, was defeated 320-0 with fifty-three abstentions. But conscription was regarded as a legitimate matter of conscience, and these abstentions were not taken so seriously.)

Crossman and his colleagues—like Henry Wallace in the United States—had publicly disputed the foreign policy of the leaders of their own party. (Wallace sent a telegram of greetings to a group of M.P.'s involved in the revolt.) Some of the effects of the "stab in the back" were similar to the consequences of the Wallace incident. Despite official efforts to minimize the rebels' importance (both Attlee and Bevin flaunted their disdain for their critics), the incident did embarrass the government and confuse both friends and adversaries abroad.

Perhaps more important, though much less obvious, was the rebellion's effect on Attlee and Bevin themselves. In the most relaxed circumstances, politicians can sometimes accept criticism constructively. But criticism as pointed and threatening as Crossman's amendment to the address has another effect. Almost invariably, the victim of such an attack feels compelled to defend his position more vigorously than before. This may explain Attlee's willingness to compare Czarist and Communist Russian foreign policy in terms which suggested Churchill's aggressive attitude toward the Soviet Union, not Attlee's previously more relaxed position.

The rebels who had dared to doubt their government so openly in November were accepted as a new subdivision of the Labour Party.* (They had no name at the outset, but eventually became known as the "Keep Left" group for a pamphlet they published in

---

* Twenty years later, Crossman said in an interview that "the row over Palestine prompted me to move the amendment to the king's speech." He said, looking back, that policy toward Russia had been a secondary concern. Perhaps it was in Crossman's mind. But Palestine was given much less attention at this stage than was the Russian issue, which dominated Crossman's own speech opening the debate on the rebels' amendment.

the summer of 1947.) Otherwise, the "stab in the back" did little to clarify British relations with Russia.

Even inside the government the rebels had support. Dalton, quoting his diary in his memoirs, denied rumors spread by the *Daily Worker* and others that together with Bevan and Morrison he was secretly supporting the rebels, but said he was "not unsympathetic to part of their case, if only they would present it properly, and in a comradely manner."

Dalton's uncertainty was typical of many serious people—politicians, newspaper editors, and academic experts, as well as informed citizens—who could not decide what Britain should think or do about Soviet Russia in late 1946. Many opted for the vague and frankly meaningless generalizations exemplified by editorials in *The Times*. One such in November suggested that Britain's role should be to seek "with infinite patience to maintain the threefold alliance by which the war was won and of holding the balance equal between the two Great Powers with which she was, and is, associated." Experts like Anthony Eden had no remarkable ideas either. "Let the victorious powers get back to the spirit which once animated them," he recommended in a "major address" that fall.

The public had decided that it was already impossible to expect the Big Three to work happily together. Dr. Gallup asked his sample in September 1946 whether Britain, America and Russia were "still allies as they were during the war, or has that friendship disappeared?" Only 24 percent thought they were still allies; 61 percent thought the wartime friendship had disappeared or was disappearing. In the middle and upper classes, more than 70 percent were pessimistic.

The group of M.P.'s on the far left did not accept the findings of such polls. They had made foreign policy an important issue in the 1945 campaign, emphasizing Labour's ability to get along with the Soviet Union. Some of them obviously decided that the foreign policy issue had contributed to Labour's easy victory. They felt justified in asserting their point of view with the fervor that infects politicians who decide they are speaking for the people against an official prejudice. They never seemed to doubt the wisdom of their position.

The uncertainty of November was abruptly replaced by a wave of optimism in December after Molotov's sudden capitulation on the five peace treaties. The optimism was officially inspired. When Bevin docked at Southampton on his way home from New York, he told reporters: "I feel more hopeful now than I've felt since I've been foreign secretary. I can see greater understanding coming...." His report to the country on the radio a few days later was similarly sanguine, and he took the opportunity to describe Britain as "midway in geography and way of life" between the United States and the Soviet Union. He said Britain considered every question "on its merits," and did not "tie herself to anybody."

Bevin's hopeful attitude undoubtedly colored the long review of foreign policy he gave in a series of Cabinet meetings in January 1947. At one of them the foreign secretary told his colleagues that "the Germans were much more dangerous than the Russians, and soon everybody would be courting them." An American reporter in London wrote at the time that there would soon be a slight shift "East and left" in British policy as a result of the improvement in Anglo-Russian relations, which British sources were describing as "the best since the war."

Field Marshal Montgomery, then Chief of the Imperial General Staff, visited Moscow in early January, at the same time Bevin was reviewing international affairs for the Cabinet, and his meeting with Stalin must have added to the optimism in London. Montgomery found the Soviet leader friendly and relaxed. He assured Stalin that Britain and America had no plans for a military alliance against the Soviet Union. "I hoped he would believe me," Montgomery later wrote. "Stalin looked me straight in the face and said with great earnestness: 'I do believe you absolutely.' He turned to his interpreter and said: 'Tell the Field Marshal again that I believe him!'" Later in the same long meeting, Stalin remarked to Montgomery that he could tell "anyone he liked, as a matter of interest" that Russia "would welcome a military alliance with Britain and considered it was necessary." Officials in London made no secret of the pleasure with which they learned of this conversation.

Whatever pleasure they felt lasted less than a week. On January 15, five days after Montgomery's meeting with Stalin, *Pravda* published an analysis of Russia's relations with Britain which concluded: "One thing has become clear. Mr. Bevin disavows the Anglo-Soviet treaty on mutual assistance." *Pravda* had decided, more than three weeks after the fact, that when Bevin said Britain did not "tie herself to anybody" in December, he was renouncing Britain's treaty with the Soviet Union. Not surprisingly, this perverse interpretation brought dismay in London, particularly to Montgomery, who thought he had explained to Stalin that although Britain wanted to base its foreign policy on complete support for the United Nations, it would adhere to existing bilateral agreements.

Britain rejected *Pravda*'s reasoning in a note to Stalin on January 19 which hardly disguised London's distress. "The broadcast [by Bevin] was intended to show that Britain's foreign policy was not aligned in an anti-Soviet direction . . ." the note said in part. *Pravda* published this explanation on January 23, and said it was unacceptable. But on the same day, the Soviet ambassador in London delivered a note from Stalin to Bevin which took a different line: "Your message and the statement of the British Government completely explain the affair and do not leave any room for misunderstandings," wrote the Soviet leader. "It is now clear that you and I share the same viewpoint with regard to the Anglo-Soviet treaty." In the same bewildering letter, Stalin said the treaty "must be strengthened before it can be renewed." Not surprisingly, British officials were reported to be suspicious of this suggestion, and generally disillusioned. The optimism of late December and early January disappeared as quickly as it had arisen.

Nevertheless, Bevin continued to appear hopeful. Late in February, just before his departure for the Moscow meeting of foreign ministers (and at a time when the American State Department was preparing the Truman Doctrine), he told the House of Commons not to expect the Big Three to agree quickly on a final treaty with Germany, but not to despair, either. "I shall not lose my faith in the good intentions of others," he said, "no matter what they may say in their press, over their radio, or anywhere else." Concerning the Russians, he said he believed "that behind all the things they say and do, at the back of their heads they know that we have got to get cooperation and, therefore, I shall let all these attacks pass over me and go on believing in their good faith."

Perhaps Bevin was exaggerating, but he did believe that the Russians were as interested in a stable world as he, and that they would eventually have to agree on some kind of accommodation. It is doubtful, however, that he still thought Stalin and Molotov were capable of "good faith." Bevin was torn throughout 1946 and 1947 between his desire to be fair, reasonable and friendly with the Soviet Union, and his own perception of the realities of Anglo-Soviet relations. He was not going to give up hope, and he was not going to allow himself to be called unreasonable.

At the same time, Bevin never let his hopes affect the firm attitude he took on each specific issue. His outburst at the February 1946 meeting of the Security Council and his comparison of Molotov's tactics to Hitler's during the September 1945 meeting of the Council of Foreign Ministers were extreme examples of a toughness which Bevin brought to all his dealings with the Russians. He was never prepared to sacrifice British interests or even his own strong sense of justice to appease the Soviet Union. He expected fairness to be reciprocated in kind; he refused to pay for it.

Bevin was afraid of the Soviet Union and its intentions. He wanted to bring America firmly into Europe to balance Russian power on the Continent. Greece and the Middle East were important to him because of their strategic importance in regard to Russia, not because they had great intrinsic importance. He was firm with the Russians because he felt that Britain was threatened by them, but he also thought the threat was manageable. His attitude was undoubtedly colored by the fact that he had extensive personal experience with Communists, and he did not like them. He had formed a bad opinion of them years before, when fighting them in his Transport and General Workers Union.

Not all of Bevin's colleagues and subordinates understood his position. On the left, frustrated M.P.'s decided incorrectly that Bevin would line up against the Soviet Union in any circumstances. For entirely different reasons some members of the diplomatic service decided long before Bevin did that Britain had given up hope of reaching agreement with Russia on postwar problems.° Apparently, Bevin did not make that decision until the second half of 1947.°° He had not yet given up in April 1947 when he wrote Attlee from Moscow: "It looks to me as if we are getting perilously near a position in which a line-up [between East and West] is taking place." That cautious letter would have surprised those who misinterpreted Bevin's firmness as a sign that he already considered cooperation with the Soviet Union impossible.

Bevin personally determined most British foreign policy after the war. He was a strong and dominating foreign secretary who conducted Britain's relations with the rest of the world with wide powers and discretion. " 'If you have a good dog, don't bark yourself' is a good proverb, and in Mr. Bevin, I had an exceptionally good dog," Attlee has written. Attlee kept well informed, and rejected the notion that foreign affairs should be "dealt with as something quite outside the ordinary business of government," but he had great confidence in his foreign secretary.

° No Foreign Office official of that period has recorded any optimism during the war about postwar relations with the Soviet Union. Nor could any of the former officials interviewed for this book recall any optimism. Sir Maurice Peterson, ambassador to Moscow after the war, wrote in his memoirs in 1950 that there never had been any real friendship between the two countries during the war, just workable relations.

°° The evidence is persuasive that Bevin did not finally lose his optimism—or at least his hope for a settlement with Russia—until late 1947. This is the recollection of Bevin's aide in

Apart from Dalton, the rest of the Cabinet had no real influence on Bevin. (The chancellor did succeed in convincing him of the gravity of the economic situation.) "If he had the prime minister with him, and he usually made sure that he had, he knew that the Cabinet would support him," Lord Strang, one of Bevin's senior officials, has written. In the Foreign Office, Bevin referred to the Cabinet as "they." He made excellent use of his permanent officials, diplomats of the career foreign service, who found this working-class trade unionist a superb minister capable of inspiring "whole-hearted devotion."

It became popular on the far left to assume that Bevin (and therefore the ideal "socialist foreign policy") had been captured by the sinister Etonians in the diplomatic service. This was an unsuccessful attempt to explain why Bevin refused to adopt the left's point of view. Bevin's acceptance of the Foreign Office, and its acceptance of him, seems above all to have been a vivid demonstration of the fact that Englishmen of all classes tend to support the same strong values. The far left had different values, and as a result, it remained an insignificant group on the fringe of British politics.

The Foreign Office under Bevin operated in a way befitting the harried times. There was no opportunity for serious long-term planning, although early in 1947 Bevin did ask a group of officials to prepare long-range studies of British policy. Those documents will be interesting to read whenever (if ever) they are released; the officials writing them must have had a difficult time, working as they were under Bevin and a permanent undersecretary who doubted "whether we have a foreign policy."

Bevin himself had to spend many weeks at conferences during 1946–47, and when in London, he had to devote much time to negotiations with Arabs and Jews, as well as Egyptians, Greeks and others. His principal deputy, Hector McNeil, undertook most

that period, Christopher Mayhew. It is also the recorded recollection of John Wheeler-Bennett, an advisor to Bevin in 1947, who wrote in his biography of King George VI that it was November or December 1947 when Bevin decided that the Soviet Union had gone "too bloody far"—words the foreign secretary applied to a speech Molotov made at that time.

of the parliamentary duties for the Foreign Office, had important responsibility for United Nations affairs and generally remained close to the foreign secretary. Christopher Mayhew, the other politician on Bevin's staff, arrived at the Foreign Office in October 1946 with very little experience, and undertook no major tasks for several months. Bevin relied heavily on his permanent officials to deal with the many undramatic developments which—in addition to all the specific problems mentioned above—continued to require the attention of Britain's diplomats.

Bevin maintained his close relationship with Attlee by visiting with the prime minister often, and writing him personal reports from abroad. There is no indication that they ever had an important disagreement about foreign policy. Attlee was pleased with Bevin's performance as a diplomat and was grateful for his power inside the Labour party. "Only Bevin could have persuaded the party to accept an anti-Russian foreign policy," Mayhew has said. Before that was necessary, Attlee and Bevin both knew that they had to ignore opinion inside the party when they thought it was misinformed.

From the moment they took office, Attlee made it clear that Bevin alone was his foreign secretary, and only Bevin's policies had his support. A month after he became prime minister, Attlee wrote Harold Laski, then Labour party chairman: "Foreign affairs are in the capable hands of Ernest Bevin. His task is quite sufficiently difficult without the embarrassment of irresponsible statements of the kind which you are making . . . [and] a period of silence on your part would be welcome." It was a stern but typical example of Attlee's attitude toward the critics on the left wing ("I never worried about them"), and of his loyalty to Bevin.

Bevin had only two obvious weaknesses—his propensity to get too involved in a problem, which really hurt him only in regard to Palestine, and his health. He was never physically fit while foreign secretary. In late July and early August 1946 he was forced to go to bed for a rest. In the months that followed, he was almost always tired, and he appeared weak to his colleagues. He seemed especially frail during January and February. Ironically, a mild heart attack in Moscow in March 1947 forced Bevin to work less and rest more often, and it restored his health remarkably. The heart attack did not surprise those who had been working with him through the winter.

Would history have taken a different course if Bevin's health had been better? It is an intriguing question. Palestine, perhaps, would have had more and more energetic attention in January and February—the crucial months—if Bevin had had a better heart. But most of the important problems of those months had a momentum of their own which was beyond the foreign secretary's control.

Probably without knowing it and certainly without admitting it, Bevin was foreign secretary at a time when Britain was losing the ability to act meaningfully by itself, except within the shrinking empire. The policies he devised and defended actually encouraged this transition. Those who really favored an independent British foreign policy in 1946–47 were the extremists of left and right who, for utterly different reasons, wanted to keep Britain and the United States apart. But the economic realities and, more important, Bevin's perception of the political realities both pushed Britain closer and closer to America.

By disposing of India, Burma, Palestine, and eventually the commitment to Greece, Britain was disposing of all its important problems save one—Europe. In the winter of 1946–47, that problem of Europe must have seemed extremely important and difficult. But, in fact, Britain had almost no control over its eventual resolution. Very quietly, almost clandestinely, Britain relinquished its place in the front rank of nations during 1946–47. It only remained for some dramatic event to inform the world of this development.

CHAPTER V

"What is Russia up to?"
    —Senator Arthur Vandenberg,
        February 1946.

The United States' decision to enter Europe to confront and contain the Soviet Union effectively began the cold war. That decision was not made until March 1947, nineteen months after the surrender of Japan. During those nineteen months, the American people and their government reluctantly abandoned the optimistic visions of the postwar world that Franklin D. Roosevelt had left them.

The Roosevelt administration began planning for peace long before the war was over. On the assumption that a postwar economic depression was possible and perhaps likely, the United States had prepared a plan to remove international trade barriers, expand trade and—not just incidentally—make the whole world a potential market for American goods. The Roosevelt administration intended to encourage the disintegration of old colonial empires and try to eliminate old-fashioned spheres of influence. The new world order was to be governed and guaranteed by a strong United Nations organization.

But all the plans the United States devised during the war quickly lost their relevance in peacetime. Even the advantages America enjoyed over other countries, which some American officials thought would insure the success of their schemes, turned out to be ineffective. Neither American might—the monopoly on the atomic bomb—nor American wealth could persuade the

Soviet Union to join in cooperative efforts to realize Roosevelt's visions. And his visions all depended on cooperation among the major powers.

There was broad agreement in postwar America, especially by late 1946, that the Soviet Union was the villain of the piece. The international hot spots of 1946 were Germany, Eastern Europe, Trieste, Greece, Turkey, Iran, China—and all of them had one thing in common. The crisis in each—it appeared from America—was caused by the Soviet Union or her allies.* As a result, American officials became increasingly preoccupied with the Russian problem: What were the Soviet Union's motives and intentions? And how should they be dealt with?

Ideally, the second question would not have been answered until there was no doubt about the answer to the first. But this was impossible. As so often happens, American officials postponed consideration of the "long-range" problems, and dealt with particular crises as they arose. In response to a series of incidents beginning at the time of Roosevelt's death in the spring of 1945, the United States improvised a policy of "friendly firmness" toward the Soviet Union before deciding whether friendliness was in order or if firmness would be effective.

Eastern Europe provided the first occasion for an expression of American firmness. Ten days before he died, Roosevelt cabled Stalin that events in Poland since their Yalta meeting had not coincided with his expectations: "I must make it quite plain to you that any . . . solution [to the Polish problem] which would result in a thinly disguised continuance of the present [Soviet-created] Warsaw regime would be unacceptable, and would cause the people of the United States to regard the Yalta agreement as having failed."

W. Averell Harriman, then the American ambassador in Moscow and himself a participant in the Yalta meetings, was

---

* The British had a different point of view. Palestine and India—Britain's principal trouble spots during 1946–47—clearly had nothing to do with Soviet Communism. Thus viewed from London, the world did not look so black and white.

increasingly pessimistic about implementing the Yalta understandings. Before Roosevelt died Harriman sought permission to return to Washington to press his views. By the time he arrived, Harry S. Truman was president.

Harriman and virtually all Roosevelt's other advisors (the only important exception was Secretary of War Henry L. Stimson), advised the new and inexperienced president that the time had come to take a firm line with Stalin regarding Eastern Europe. The opportunity to do so arose almost immediately, when the Soviet foreign minister, V. M. Molotov, stopped in Washington to talk to Truman on his way to the first United Nations meeting in San Francisco. Truman was curt and angry when he saw Molotov. He told his guest that the Yalta agreements could be implemented if Stalin kept his word. Molotov protested that the Soviet Union believed it was respecting the agreement, but Truman cut him off.

Symbolically, at least, this was an important moment. Truman's bluster was the first occasion when the United States deliberately took a "tough" line with the Soviet Union.* This happened again more than once during 1945.

By August 1946 a "tough" attitude was the predominant one inside the Truman administration. To see how it evolved, it will be necessary to go outside the boundaries of this book for a brief review of events earlier in 1946.

The year began with the first meeting of the new United Nations Security Council, and that began with an open dispute between East and West over Iran. Britain, the United States and the Soviet Union had agreed during the war that all foreign troops should be out of Iran six months after the war ended—*i.e.,* by March 1946. Toward the end of the war, Soviet troops occupying

* It has been argued that Truman's brusque exchanges with Molotov demonstrated that the new president had abandoned his predecessor's foreign policy. Similar claims were made a generation later about Lyndon B. Johnson and John F. Kennedy's Vietnam policies. The important fact in both cases is that the new presidents followed the advice of their predecessors' advisors, and believed they were adhering to established policies. All the available evidence confirms that Truman was determined to maintain Roosevelt's policies. Harriman, for one, believes Roosevelt would have acted much as Truman did had he lived longer.

Iranian Azerbaijan, a northern province along the Soviet border, helped establish a semiautonomous local government composed of Iranians sympathetic to Soviet interests.

In November 1945 the Iranian government in Teheran received reports of a revolt in Azerbaijan, and tried to send its troops into the province. Soviet forces refused to let them in. Britain immediately accused the Soviet Union of breaking the wartime agreements that protected Iran's sovereignty. The United States tried to mediate. In December the foreign ministers considered the dispute in Moscow, but without result. Iran was impatient for action, and decided to press its case before the first meeting of the Security Council.

The United States was apprehensive about this development. It was recognized in Washington that a debate at the United Nations about Iran would reveal publicly a serious division between the Soviet Union and the United States and Britain. A strong group inside the State Department sought to minimize the Iranian issue and to resolve it privately with the Russians, avoiding the embarrassment of an open display of disaffection at the Security Council's first meeting. But after long and heated discussions, it was decided to debate the dispute openly. The United States supported the Iranian complaint.

Britain was also reluctant to advertise the differences between Russia and the West, but agreed when it became clear that Iran was determined to press its case. The Russians were furious, and responded by accusing Britain of interference in Greece and Indonesia. (These charges led to Bevin's outburst against Molotov and the Soviet Union in February.) When Iran's complaint came before the Security Council, the Soviet delegate argued that it should not even be considered. When he lost that fight, he defended Soviet policy in Iran and denied any intervention in its affairs, though he did not deny that the Iranian government's troops had been kept out of Azerbaijan. While the Security Council argued, a new government came to power in Iran under a premier known to favor an accommodation with the Russians.

This government said it would negotiate directly with the Soviet Union. The Security Council gave its blessing to this turn of events on January 30.

These negotiations made no real progress. The Russians insisted on recognition for the autonomy of Azerbaijan, on some rights over oil in northern Iran, and on continued presence of Soviet troops in various parts of the country. On March 1, the agreed date for all foreign troops to leave Iran, the Soviet Union announced that "some troops" would remain in Iran "until the situation has been elucidated." This blatant renunciation of previous promises brought strong protests from London and Washington. An American note delivered March 6 said the United States "cannot remain indifferent" to Russia's retention of troops in Iran, and expressed "the earnest hope that the Government of the Soviet Union will do its part to promote peace by withdrawing immediately all Soviet forces from the territory of Iran." Britain sent a similar message.

On March 8, having heard nothing from Moscow, the Americans sent a second stern note. (By this time the State Department had received reports from Iran that Soviet troops appeared to be moving toward Teheran.) The situation remained tense until March 24, when Moscow Radio announced that all Soviet troops would leave Iran within six weeks, unless the situation there changed significantly.

But the Russians did not repeat this assurance formally to Iran, Britain or the United States, so Iran continued to press its case in the U.N. The Soviets tried to postpone consideration of the Iranian complaint, but the other members of the Security Council (except Poland) voted to hear it at once. Andrei Gromyko, the Soviet delegate, then walked out of the meeting. For a moment it was feared that the Soviet Union had abandoned the United Nations. In fact, Gromyko was only hoping to extend the veto to procedural questions by boycotting debates on subjects which the Russians had not approved.

Withdrawal of Soviet troops did not end the dispute, but it did end the crisis. In April the Soviet Union and Iran signed a new agreement. It gave the Russians the right to develop some of Iran's oil reserves in partnership with the Iranian government. Iran also promised to recognize the autonomy of the Azerbaijan regime in local matters, if the rebels respected the ultimate authority of the central government. In December 1946, after Soviet troops had withdrawn, the central government entered Azerbaijan without difficulty and the local government collapsed, to the great pleasure of its constituents.

The Iranian incident was a turning point in the history of American policy. It was the first open fight with the Soviet Union, and the first occasion that America took an overtly "tough" stand. The United States had chosen not to hide a serious disagreement with the Soviet Union. The incident suggested that a firm policy would be successful—a boost for those in the State Department who had been confident of this for some time. But it was not an irrevocable precedent for the future.

Several other developments in the midst of the struggle over Iran suggested even at the time that a significant shift in American policy was occurring. In February, apparently convinced that the Soviet threat to Iran was, indirectly, a threat to neighboring Turkey, Truman decided to send the body of the Turkish ambassador to Washington home to Turkey on the battleship *Missouri*. It was hardly a spontaneous act; the ambassador had been dead for more than a year. The ship left America on March 21. At a time when tensions in the Middle East were obvious and serious, its mission seemed unmistakably political. Sending the *Missouri* to the Mediterranean was the first use of American power in the war of nerves with the Soviet Union. (The ship also visited Greece.)

But there had been some hesitation in Washington about such a show of strength. An earlier plan to accompany the *Missouri* with a large escort of other warships was dropped.* And the an-

---

* Forrestal related the decision to drop the escort to Churchill, who was then in Washington. Churchill was disappointed. Forrestal recorded his comment "that a gesture of power not fully implemented was almost less effective than no gesture at all."

nouncement of the *Missouri's* mission was accompanied by a denial that it had any political importance.

If the Soviet Union felt any similar anxiety, it was not evident that February. On February 9, the eve of elections for the Supreme Soviet, Stalin delivered a fierce oration which caused great alarm in the United States and elsewhere. He described the Second World War "as the result of the development of economic and political spheres on the basis of monopolistic capitalism," and he did not indicate that he thought the war had purged capitalism of its sins. "The capitalist system of world economy conceals in itself the elements of general crisis and military classes," he said.

He announced fantastic targets for Soviet heavy industry, and profusely praised the Red Army, whose success in the war put the lie to "foreign journalists" who thought Russian society could not hold together under stress. He said the Soviet Union would prepare "to guarantee our country against any eventuality." He also promised a better life for Russia's citizens and more consumer goods, but these passages, tucked away near the end of the speech, were largely ignored in the West.

James Forrestal, Truman's Secretary of the Navy and a consistent advocate of a hard line against the Soviet Union, was deeply impressed by the speech and cited it often in the following months. He was by no means alone. Justice William O. Douglas, a liberal member of the Supreme Court, described Stalin's oration as "the Declaration of World War III." Byrnes later wrote that the speech was a "shock to me." It was not forgotten in the United States.

A week before Stalin spoke, the State Department in Washington, apparently bewildered by Soviet behavior, asked the American embassy in Moscow to explain it. George F. Kennan, who had devoted most of his career to studying the Soviet Union, was then in charge of the Moscow embassy, and jumped at the chance to offer his own strong opinions. (Kennan had been offering them for months in other reports and cables, apparently without much result.) He hurriedly produced the long telegram that has become one of the most celebrated documents in American diplomatic history—a document that startled and pleased official Washington when it arrived on February 23. Kennan's analysis is best summarized by his own recapitulation:

> ... We have here a political force committed fanatically to the belief that with the United States there can be no permanent *modus vivendi*, that it is desirable and necessary that the internal harmony of our society be disrupted, our traditional way of life be destroyed, the international authority of our state be broken, if Soviet power is to be secure. This political force has complete power of disposition over energies of one of world's greatest peoples and resources of world's richest national territory, and is borne along by deep and powerful currents of Russian nationalism. In addition, it has an elaborate and far flung apparatus for exertion of its influence in other countries, an apparatus of amazing flexibility and versatility, managed by people whose experience and skill in underground methods are presumably without parallel in history. Finally, it is seemingly inaccessible to considerations of reality in its basic reactions. For it, the vast fund of objective fact about human society is not, as with us, the measure against which outlook is constantly being tested and re-formed, but a grab bag from which individual items are selected arbitrarily and tendentiously to bolster an outlook already preconceived. . . . Problem of how to cope with this force is undoubtedly greatest task our diplomacy has ever faced and probably it will ever have to face. . . .

Kennan's cable arrived at a time when the American Secretary of State, James F. Byrnes, was in political trouble. Byrnes was a proud man who wanted to run American foreign policy by himself. As a result, he was losing the confidence of his chief, President Truman, and the support of the Republican party, which had endorsed first Roosevelt's and then Truman's foreign policies throughout the war.

Byrnes was criticized on two points: the president was unhappy that he acted so independently, and reported so sparsely and vaguely to Washington when working overseas. The Republicans (and to some extent Truman too) were disturbed by Byrnes's readiness to compromise with the Soviet Union. The Republicans' leading spokesman on foreign affairs, Senator Arthur Vandenberg, was pessimistic about any cooperation with Russia, and was one of several important figures who began to pressure Byrnes to deal with the Russians more firmly.

Not that Byrnes had been a pushover for the Soviet Union. In the very first foreign ministers' meeting he attended, the new secretary had been tough and uncompromising. But later he had showed a willingness to trade off with the Russians, rather in the manner of the courthouse politics of his native South Carolina. Vandenberg and others (including diplomats like Kennan, who was upset by Byrnes's flexibility in Moscow in December 1945) thought that the courthouse was a bad analogy for relations with Joseph Stalin. Vandenberg once wrote privately that he mistrusted Byrnes because "his whole life has been a career of compromise."

In late 1945 and early 1946, Republican politicians were increasingly inclined to speak out against Byrnes's compromising attitude, suggesting that foreign policy could become an issue in the 1946 congressional elections. Vandenberg and John Foster Dulles, the Republicans' other leading spokesman on foreign affairs, accompanied Byrnes to the London meeting of the United Nations General Assembly in January 1946. When they returned to Washington in mid-February, both were angry with Byrnes (who apparently paid little attention to them or their opinions during the meeting). Reports appeared in the press that both might refuse to join any future delegations led by the secretary of state.

Vandenberg advertised his discontent on February 27 in a Senate speech which posed that timely question, "What is Russia up to now?" He concluded that the United States was not pressing its position with sufficient firmness. Coexistence with the Russians,

Vandenberg said, would be possible only "if the United States speaks just as plainly upon all occasions as Russia does. . . ." It was time to draw a line, he said, beyond which there could be no further compromises.

The next day, Byrnes made a major address to the Overseas Press Club in New York. This stern speech, he wrote later, marked a significant change in his attitude toward Russia.* He told the assembled journalists: ". . . The Charter [of the United Nations] forbids aggression, and we cannot allow aggression to be accomplished by coercion or pressure or by subterfuge such as political infiltration. . . . We will not and we cannot stand aloof if force or threat of force is used contrary to the purposes and principles of the Charter." Byrnes left no doubt as to whom he was talking about. No nation, he said, was entitled to station troops on the territory of another country (*i.e.*, Iran) without consent; no nation could be allowed to delay making peace indefinitely; no nation could seize reparations from former enemies before the Allies had reached formal agreement on reparations. The United States could not ignore "a unilateral gnawing away at the status quo. . . ."

In the two weeks that followed Byrnes's speech, John Foster Dulles and Senator Tom Connally of Texas, both delegates with Byrnes at the London General Assembly meeting in January, spoke out in similar terms. And then, louder than any of these, came the resonant voice of Winston Churchill, who delivered his

* This admission that the Overseas Press Club speech represented a new attitude toward Russia is one piece of evidence in an interesting mystery. Truman wrote in his memoirs that he was unhappy with Byrnes's performance at the Moscow meeting of foreign ministers, and unhappy with his behavior when he returned home. Truman recorded that he "wrote a letter in longhand" to Byrnes which amounted to a detailed criticism of the secretary's behavior. It was also a declaration of policy. According to his memoirs, Truman wrote: "there isn't a doubt in my mind that Russia intends an invasion of Turkey and the seizure of the Black Sea straits to the Mediterranean. Unless Russia is faced with an iron fist and strong language, another war is in the making." The letter concluded, "I'm tired of babying the Soviets." According to the memoirs, Truman called Byrnes to his office and read him this 1000-word document aloud.

Byrnes denied that this incident took place. "Of course," he told his sympathetic famous "iron curtain" speech at Fulton, Missouri, on March 5, 1946 (the day before the Soviet Union received the first strongly worded American note on Iran).

Churchill established a new standard of brusqueness at Fulton with his pessimistic analysis of events in Europe. In one somber sentence he coined a phrase that would dominate an era: "From Stettin in the Baltic to Trieste in the Adriatic an iron curtain has descended across the continent of Europe." Churchill would make no predictions: "Nobody knows what Soviet Russia and its communist international organization intends to do in the immediate future, or what are the limits, if any, to their expansive and proselytizing tendencies." However, he did perceive that "in a great number of countries, far from the Russian frontiers and throughout the world, communist fifth columns are established and work in complete unity and absolute obedience to the directions they receive from the communist center." And he thought he knew Russia's immediate goal: "What they desire is the fruits of war and the indefinite expansion of their power and doctrines, though without war itself." And he suggested a way to cope with this threat: "From what I have seen of our Russian friends and allies during the war, I am convinced that there is nothing they admire so much as strength, and there is nothing for which they have less respect than for military weakness." Strength, he thought, should be put at the disposal of the United Nations.

---

biographer, George Curry, "such a letter was never sent to me nor read to me. Had this occurred . . . I would have resigned immediately."

Who told the truth? Truman's later split with Byrnes obviously colored all the president's recollections of him, even of times when they were working together. There are enough other errors and self-serving sections in Truman's memoirs to allow for the possibility that Byrnes's memory is the accurate one. If Truman was as angry with Byrnes as this anecdote suggests, he disguised the anger well when he praised Byrnes's Moscow performance publicly several times that same month. There is no other hint in the available documents that Truman was actually anticipating a Soviet attack on Turkey and the Black Sea straits. Nor is there evidence that Truman did anything to "stop babying the Soviets." Six weeks later, though, he told Admiral William D. Leahy that he was dissatisfied with the policy of appeasing the Russians and would take a stronger position. Still, nothing was actually done in this spirit until the firm notes to Moscow over Iran, in early March.

Furthermore, the English-speaking nations would have to cooperate to protect free nations from communism.

Churchill's vivid speech was both evocative and provocative, and not entirely candid. The existence of an "iron curtain" could hardly have surprised Churchill; he invited it in October 1944, when he conceded most of the Balkans to Stalin's influence in return for British predominance in Greece. The former prime minister's willingness to speak so bluntly surprised and angered many people throughout the world. Stalin quickly gave an interview to *Pravda* in which he stated: ". . . Mr. Churchill and his friends bear a striking resemblance to Hitler and his friends."

The popular reaction to the Fulton speech in the United States was generally cautious and sometimes hostile. Americans were not prepared for a full-blown confrontation with the Soviet Union; nor were they interested in any alliance with Britain. Truman's presence on the platform while Churchill spoke must have appeared to be an endorsement of his views, especially to the Russians. The president tried to discourage such speculation. He let it be known that he did not agree with all that Churchill had said. In a press conference three days after the speech, Byrnes said the United States had nothing to do with Churchill's speech, and refused to support his views. Byrnes's deputy, Dean Acheson, pointedly absented himself from a dinner in Churchill's honor in New York. A week after the speech at his regular press conference, Truman refused to make any substantive comment on it.

In fact, both Byrnes and Truman knew more than they were willing to admit. The secretary of state had heard an outline of the speech from Churchill in mid-February. A day or two before it was delivered, Churchill read him the entire document. Byrnes subsequently gave the president a resumé, so that Truman could honestly say that he had not read the speech if it later caused trouble. But according to Churchill, he showed Truman his text on the train to Missouri. "He told me that he thought it was admirable and would do nothing but good though it would make a stir." Churchill said Truman "seemed equally pleased before and

136

after." Byrnes and Admiral William Leahy also read and liked the speech, according to Churchill. There had been private collaboration with Churchill which Truman never admitted. The president had used the former prime minister to send up that effective political weapon, a trial balloon.

That did not mean that Truman was as pessimistic as Churchill about relations with the Soviet Union. The president remained cautious, probing and uncertain. The United States was not prepared to commit itself to an active anti-Soviet or anti-Communist foreign policy. The reliability of Byrnes's promise that America "will not and . . . cannot stand aloof" in the face of aggression or subversion was not yet confirmed by any action. As recently as early February, the American delegate to the United Nations, Edward Stettinius, had sat through a debate on aggression in Greece without saying a word. The State Department's query to Kennan in Moscow on February 3 indicates that Washington was then just beginning to consider carefully what Russia was "up to."

The situation moved rapidly after that. The coincidence of Kennan's telegram, increasing Republican pressure on Byrnes, the secretary's own declaration of firmness, then Churchill's speech and the notes on Iran indicate a momentous period in American diplomatic history. But it was a period in which the inclinations and opinions of statesmen were out of harmony both with their own capabilities and the mood of the country. Had the Truman administration followed its new tough line to its logical consequences, the United States would have undertaken an interventionist foreign policy around the periphery of Soviet power to prevent its further expansion. But the Truman administration had neither the resources nor the popular support for that kind of policy. In the spring of 1946, the American public clamored for a return to "normalcy," a condition of uncertain definition, but certainly a condition which precluded any new foreign adventures.

In April the new American ambassador to Moscow, General

Walter Bedell Smith, met with Stalin for two hours. At the outset Smith asked Stalin, "How far is Russia going to go?" Instead of a direct answer, he got a long review of many issues. At one point Stalin said he believed that the United States and Britain were joined in an alliance to thwart the Soviet Union.° At the end of the interview the ambassador returned to his original question. Stalin finally answered, "We're not going much further." Did that mean Turkey? Stalin recalled that he had told Truman he would not attack Turkey. "But Turkey is weak, and the Soviet Union is very conscious of the danger of foreign control of the [Black Sea] Straits, which Turkey is not strong enough to protect."

In late April Byrnes suggested a twenty-five-year treaty among the Big Four guaranteeing the demilitarization of Germany within the framework of the United Nations. It was a suggestion which had much support in the United States, but at the time the Soviet Union paid no attention to it. In May the United States cancelled further deliveries of reparations from its zone to the Soviet zone in Germany. In June Washington learned of the remarkable interview that Maxim Litvinov, then the Soviet Union's deputy foreign minister, had given to Richard C. Hottelet of C.B.S. news. Litvinov blamed his own country for East-West tensions, and predicted that if the United States relented to then-current Soviet demands, it would soon face a new set of demands.

The summer was uneventful, but conditions did not improve. By August 1946 there was little doubt in Washington that the Russians were constantly seeking to extend their influence ("to advance the limits of Soviet power," as Kennan had put it six months before). At least there was no evidence to the contrary.

Until August America had defended her interests with strong language over Iran and the cancellation of reparations shipments in Germany. Strong language could be used again. But what if something more were needed? Cancelling the delivery of reparations had been easy enough, because America had both power and responsibility in its zone of Germany. But the U.S. had neither in

° Three months earlier, Stalin assured Field Marshall Montgomery that he realized Britain and America were *not* alligned against the Soviet Union.

most of the rest of Europe, the Middle East or Asia outside Japan.

The Soviet Union had an obvious and longstanding interest in Turkey's Straits of Bosphorus and the Dardanelles. These vital waterways were the only sea route connecting an immense area of Russia with the rest of the world. In 1915 the czar had been promised control over the Straits after the First World War, but the Bolsheviks repudiated that (and all other) agreements after taking power in 1917. Truman also thought that the Straits and Turkey generally were of great strategic importance. He also believed that the United States should try to help all nations, especially little ones, to govern themselves without interference from other states. This policy was not universally applied. It was forgotten in Eastern Europe, where Russia's interference could have been prevented only by removing Russia's presence. But a state like Turkey, both free and strategically important, seemed to qualify for America's full support.

That support was tested in early August when the Soviet Union outlined its proposals for the future of the Straits in a note to the American government. The Russians suggested that the Straits be governed by a regime chosen by Turkey and the other Black Sea powers (Rumania, Bulgaria and the U.S.S.R.), and that Russia and Turkey "organize joint means of defense of the Straits." In effect, the Soviet Union sought to eliminate the influence of all the Western powers from the Dardanelles, and to force the Turks to accept Russian military "aid." Turkey bitterly opposed both propositions.

On August 14 a committee which included Acheson (then the acting secretary of state), Forrestal, and Kenneth C. Royall, the undersecretary of war, considered the implications of the Soviet note. They agreed that it should be rejected in the strongest terms. The next afternoon the committee met President Truman at the White House. Acheson reviewed the conclusions reached the day before. He said that a firm response was necessary because "these [Russian] demands would be followed next by infiltration and domination of Greece . . . with the obvious threat to the Middle East. . . ." He warned that if the Russians refused to back down, an armed conflict was possible. He also reported the committee's recommendations that American warships visit the Eastern Mediterranean as a demonstration of U.S. support for Turkey.

Truman quickly approved Acheson's suggestions, observing that "we might as well find out whether the Russians [are] bent on world conquest now as in five or ten years." Eisenhower, then Army Chief of Staff, leaned toward Acheson and whispered too loudly, "Do you think he knows what he's doing? This could mean war!" Like a schoolteacher, Truman turned to Acheson and asked, "What did he say to you?" Acheson replied that Eisenhower had wondered if the president knew what he was doing. Truman then invited the group to gather round his desk. He opened a large map of the eastern Mediterranean area and delivered a fifteen-minute lecture on its significance throughout most of recorded history. "Well, Ike, do I know what I'm doing?" Truman asked when he was finished. The general agreed that he did.*

On August 19 Acheson handed the American reply to the Soviet chargé d'affaires in Washington. It left no doubt about America's position. The United States could not agree that only the Black Sea powers should govern the Straits. It was America's "firm opinion" that "Turkey should continue to be primarily responsible for the defense of the Straits. Should the Straits become an object of attack or threat of attack by an aggressor, the resulting situation would . . . clearly be a matter for action on the part of the Security Council of the United Nations."

Byrnes, then in Paris, apparently told Bevin on August 17 of America's planned reaction. Bevin said he approved the stern reply, but could not identify Britain with it without consulting with his colleagues in London. He must have persuaded Attlee that a tough note was in order, for Britain delivered one to the Russians on August 21. The next day Turkey followed with its own categorical rejection. In early September, the giant carrier *Franklin D. Roosevelt*, accompanied by five other ships, sailed into

---

* This story was recalled by Dean Acheson in an interview in 1966. A more restrained version of the story appears in Acheson's memoirs.

the eastern Mediterranean. The Russians did not press the issue, although in late September they brought it up again in another note to Turkey. The United States again answered on behalf of the Turks, and repeated that Russia's proposals were unacceptable. That was the end of the incident.

The Straits dispute coincided with Yugoslavia's attacks on the two American aircraft, and at the time, the more vivid encounter with the Yugoslavs obscured the importance of the note to Moscow on the Dardanelles. The aggressive Marshal Tito and his blatantly unreasonable behavior made much bigger headlines than the more subtle note regarding the Straits. America's forty-eight-hour ultimatum to Tito, which followed the Straits note by only two days, was the most dramatic event in the postwar period until that time. But as an indication of the future of American policy, the note on the Straits was much more important. (In contrast to Truman's close involvement in preparing the note on the Straits, the president was cruising on the presidential yacht *Williamsburg* when Byrnes, in Paris, drafted the note to Yugoslavia.) Obviously, when two American airplanes were shot down without provocation and their passengers held as prisoners, the U.S. government had to react swiftly and sternly.

The question of the Straits was hardly so simple. The United States could not have decided lightly to defend Turkey's right to control the Straits alone. Unless it was to be an isolated instance, that decision implied an important new commitment to the restraint of Soviet Russia.

Truman appeared to have made this new commitment, but without great resolve. The president and his aides had not undertaken the preparations that would have been necessary to support their new position. Militarily, there were virtually no contingency plans for the possibility of an armed conflict in Europe or elsewhere (although U.S. forces were alerted when the notes to Russia and Yugoslavia were sent). Forrestal told Acheson on August 23 that he was "very apprehensive about our capabilities to meet any sudden emergency in Europe." This apprehension was shared throughout the military establishment. Sending warships to the eastern Mediterranean was an impressive gesture, but it was an inadequate substitute for military planning.

Nor did the decision (which resulted from the two crises in August) to initiate military staff discussions with the British in Washington constitute coordinated planning. When those talks began in late August, it was discovered that "no very definite plans [for an Anglo-American response to a military crisis in Europe] had been evolved because no one had raised the question," according to U.S. Admiral D.C. Ramsey, a participant in the discussions. And military preparations were only one of the prerequisites to a meaningful policy of "containment." Painful changes in America's economic and diplomatic policies would also be required.

But in August 1946 President Truman was compelled to make painful decisions of a very different kind. The continuing pressures of inflation had persuaded the president, as he said in early August, that "we must do everything in our power" to reduce spending. He presented an extraordinary budget message promising that government expenditure would be reduced by $2.2 billion. $1.65 billion would be cut from the defense budget.

Truman was responding to economic necessity and to the mood of that August, when domestic politics outweighed international affairs, not only for the American public, but for the president, too.° His attitude toward the armed forces suggested such priorities. In August, when Truman announced these new reductions in the defense establishment, America's forces had already fallen from an average strength of 11.6 million men and women in 1945 to fewer than 2.5 million in August 1946. (As a result of Truman's budget-cutting, the number continued to fall to less than two

---

° According to a poll taken in September 1946, only 23 percent of the American public thought that foreign policy issues were the most important problems facing the United States at that time.

million by the end of 1946.)* These were not routine, previously anticipated reductions; the chiefs of staff found it extremely difficult to make the cuts that the president ordered in August.

August 1946 was the beginning of the bleakest period of Truman's presidency. IIis authority was weak, his morale low and his horizons narrow. It was not a time for making momentous decisions about the future of the world.

Perhaps the most accurate indication of the president's position was the Wallace affair. Wallace certainly understood that his colleagues in the cabinet were increasingly attracted to a tough policy toward the Soviet Union. He fervently opposed such a policy. Truman had been aware of his views since March 1946, and vividly aware of them since July, when Wallace had written him a single-spaced, twelve-page memorandum advocating a conciliatory policy. Truman did not see Wallace personally from early August until September 10. (There was only one cabinet meeting in those weeks, and Wallace missed it.) They met briefly on September 10, and Wallace showed Truman the speech he planned to make in New York two days later. The president thumbed through it, perhaps reading a paragraph or two, but apparently no more. He told Wallace it sounded fine.

Advance copies were distributed to the press on the morning of the speech, but no one in the government outside Wallace's Department of Commerce read a copy until that afternoon. Apparently the first official to notice it was James W. Riddleberger, acting head of the Office of European Affairs in the State Department. He showed it to his colleague, Loy Henderson, and the two of them took it to Will Clayton, then acting secretary of state. John L. Sullivan, undersecretary of the Navy, was in

---

* The eagerness with which Americans sought to bring the boys home after the war cannot be exaggerated. As early as the summer and fall of 1944, Thomas Dewey found that the only issue he could use effectively against Roosevelt was the rumor that FDR had a secret plan to keep large numbers of Americans under arms after the war. Roosevelt had to make a special statement denying that he had any such intention. After that, Americans only grew more anxious to demobilize their army.

Clayton's office with an aide, and the entire group agreed that the speech would seriously compromise Secretary Byrnes, and that at least some sections of it should be deleted. They were especially upset by the sentence Wallace added after seeing Truman, claiming that the president had endorsed his views.

Clayton was persuaded to call the White House, where he talked to Charles Ross, Truman's press secretary. Clayton complained to Ross about Wallace's speech, but Sullivan felt he was being too meek about it, and took the phone. Sullivan emphasized what effect the speech might have, but the press secretary apparently felt the matter was settled. (Well he might have, after hearing Truman's positive comments on the speech at his press conference that same afternoon, when the president had said emphatically that he had read Wallace's remarks, found them fully reconcilable with his administration's foreign policy, and had "approved the whole speech.") When the bomb struck, the White House was not in its shelter.

Wallace's speech "turned out to be a different kind than the president had thought," as one of Truman's aides later put it. Wallace did change his speech slightly as he delivered it. When the 19,000 people in Madison Square Garden reacted harshly to some mild criticism of the Soviet Union, Wallace deleted two other passages critical of the Russians as he came to them. And he added extemporaneously, "I realize that the danger of war is much less from Communism than it is from Imperialism." But these changes made only a small difference. The most damaging things Wallace said were in the draft which the president thumbed through.

Two sentences stood out. "We have no more business in the political affairs of Eastern Europe than Russia has in the political affairs of Latin America, Western Europe and the United States," Wallace suggested at one point. And in an obvious reference to Byrnes's firm attitude, Wallace said, "We are reckoning with a force which cannot be handled successfully by a 'get tough with Russia' policy." Was this the speech that the president had per-

sonally approved? The most charitable observers thought the
president must have made an awful mistake; others thought he
had decided to change the course of American policy completely.

In Paris, Byrnes and his aides were appalled. Clayton had informed the secretary of the contents of Wallace's speech and his
own and Sullivan's protest to Ross in a cable which Byrnes
received the morning after Wallace spoke. Clayton and Donald S.
Russell, Byrnes's closest assistant in the State Department, kept
their chief informed of the bizarre developments of the affair as
they occurred.

Two days after the speech, Truman called a press conference to
say that he had made a mistake—he hadn't really endorsed
Wallace's views, but only his right to express them. This satisfied
no one. Benjamin Cohen, who was with Byrnes in Paris, has
recalled that the American delegation there was prepared to
believe almost anything about the meaning of the incident. "You
couldn't be sure about the relations between Truman and his
advisors in those days," according to Cohen.

Byrnes was ready to resign, as he cabled to Washington more
than once during the inconclusive days after the speech. He also
prepared a statement, which in the end was never used, con-
tradicting Wallace's accusation that the United States was pursuing a "get tough with Russia" policy in collaboration with
Britain. "I assert that the president and I have been looking
abroad through our own American eyes and not through either the
eyes of the British Foreign Office or an anti-Russian press, and any
statement or intimation to the contrary is absolutely untrue,"
Byrnes would have said, if he had thought it necessary to release
the statement.*

While the administration's position remained confused,
Wallace released the long letter he had written Truman in July,
suggesting, among other things, that the United States should
reduce spending on armaments, and share the secret of the atomic

* George Curry's biography of Byrnes contains quotations from this document that was
never used. Curry had access to Byrnes's private files.

bomb with the Soviet Union. On September 18 Truman finally called Wallace to his office. They talked for two and a half hours, and at the end of the meeting Wallace reluctantly promised to make no more speeches on foreign policy until after the Paris Peace Conference. But Wallace's attitude upset Truman. He was even more upset when he learned that Wallace told a number of other people about his long meeting with the president.

Not until September 19, a week after the speech, did the president talk with Byrnes. Telephone connections were bad, so they conversed by teletype. Byrnes had the first word—indeed, the first 1200 words, in which he argued that America could not allow the world to doubt its resolution. He concluded: "You and I spent fifteen months building a bipartisan foreign policy. We did a fine job convincing the world that it was a permanent policy upon which the world could rely. Wallace destroyed it in a day." Truman's reply was reassuring: nothing had changed, their policy was intact, nobody appreciated the excellent job Byrnes was doing more than he did. "I shall continue to support you with everything I have," Truman promised. The next day the president asked Wallace for his resignation.*

When it was finally over, no one was quite sure what had happened, or why. James Reston wrote ruefully of "the most astounding and disturbing series of errors to come out of the White House in a generation," and he could not be contradicted.**
Such blundering was not typical of Harry Truman, but it revealed

* Cabell Phillips, whose book *The Truman Presidency* was written with the help of several important members of the Truman administration, wrote that when Truman finally decided to fire Wallace, he drafted a vituperative letter in longhand to the secretary of commerce and sent it to him by messenger. According to Phillips, Truman's staff was unaware of this letter until Wallace himself called Charles Ross and read him some of the president's heated prose. Wallace thought this ill-considered communication might be a liability in history, and Ross agreed. Wallace sent the document to the White House, and Ross destroyed it. All that remains is a very polite and brief correspondence between Truman and Wallace, the secretary offering his resignation and the president accepting it.

** Clifford and Ross found some consolation in the episode. It helped them persuade the president to organize the staff work in the White House more carefully, and to be sure he knew all sides of an issue before making a decision.

his predicament. He was uncertain of his position, both in Washington and in the country. Wallace was a leader of the nation's intellectual left, a group Truman thought was important to the Democratic party, especially when congressional elections were less than two months away. Wallace delivered his controversial speech in New York, an important state for the Democrats at any time, and especially important in 1946, when Thomas E. Dewey was running for reelection to the governorship. Dewey was one of the most obvious possibilities for the Republican presidential nomination in 1948.

Harried by domestic affairs (a national maritime strike was then occupying much of the president's attention) and aware of his —and the Democrats'—declining popularity, Truman was not eager to acknowledge a serious division inside his cabinet, or to take sides in an intraparty argument. The president was so reluctant to resolve the impossible situation which the speech created that he waited seven days before even speaking to Wallace. It required an eighth day for the president to make the decision which he would have made on the first, if diplomatic considerations had been paramount.

But diplomatic considerations were not so important. Had they been, the Wallace incident probably would not have occurred, and it certainly would have been less painful. The official reaction to Wallace's speech proved, on one level, that the speech itself was incorrect—clearly, the administration was not committed to an active "get tough with Russia" policy. If Truman really felt such a commitment, Wallace could not have remained in the cabinet for eight days after making his speech. And the president's press secretary could not have failed to react to the pointed comments of Undersecretary of the Navy, John L. Sullivan, when he protested about Wallace's speech a few hours before it was delivered.

The fact was that at the operative level, the Truman administration was confused and uncertain in September. The strong note to Russia on the Straits had been an important stage in the evolution of American policy, but the Wallace incident showed that the full implications of that note had not yet been accepted. The American people and the nations of the world still did not know what United States foreign policy was. Mr. Low, watching these events from London, drew a cartoon at the time of Wallace's resignation picturing "U.S. Statesmanship" reaching for the chalice of "world leadership and responsibility," but held back by the "child minds." It was captioned, "Touch and Go."

The situation was not so delicate as Mr. Low thought. Undeniably, the Wallace episode was a blow to the credibility of American policy. Mr. Low could justifiably wonder if the United States had a consistent foreign policy. But inside the government, the incident cleared the air. It was the last important struggle within the administration about an issue related to foreign policy in 1946–47.

Wallace himself was the last important member of the Truman cabinet who believed that demonstrations of American friendship could mollify the Soviet Union. (He was replaced as secretary of commerce by W. Averell Harriman, who had decided eighteen months earlier that the Russians could not be trusted.) By dismissing Wallace, Truman created a new situation in which "Truman's policy" was firm toward Russia, but the policy of Truman's critics was conciliatory, or even apologetic. Previously, the president had made room in his cabinet for both a Byrnes and a Wallace; such broadmindedness was not evident after September 1946.

There was no similar incident again. Perhaps the Wallace affair was a necessary jolt. Until Wallace articulated the differences between the administration's foreign policy and the views of the left wing he represented, the public had not realized how fundamental those differences were. And until Truman was compelled to chose between his foreign policy and the left wing of his party, the administration itself tended to confuse issues it should have been clarifying.

Wallace's speech and its aftermath did help clarify both the president's position and American foreign policy. Another important but secret development may have helped the president even more. Several weeks before the Wallace incident, Mr. Truman asked Clark M. Clifford, one of his most influential aides, to study America's relations with the Soviet Union in detail. He instructed Clifford to talk with virtually every important figure in the American government; military officers, diplomats, intelligence experts and anyone else with expert advice or an opinion on U.S.-Soviet relations. Clifford's report was being drafted during the days of the furor over the Wallace speech. He handed it to the president on September 24.

Clifford's memorandum, nearly 20,000 words long, included a review of Soviet-American relations during and after the war, an analysis of Soviet behavior in that period and recommendations for future American policy. Its tone was grave and uncompromising. "The fundamental tenet of the communist philosophy embraced by Soviet leaders is that the peaceful coexistence of communist and capitalist nations is impossible," Clifford wrote near the outset. "The defenders of the communist faith, as the present Soviet leaders regard themselves, assume that conflict between the Soviet Union and the leading capitalist powers is inevitable. . . ." This was an important thesis of Kennan's telegram of the previous February. He meant, in other words, that the United States could not appease the Soviet Union because the Soviet leaders believed in the inevitability of war with the United States.

But like Kennan, Clifford also found some cause for optimism, provided that America was resolute. The Russians, Clifford concluded, "want to postpone the conflict [with capitalism] for many years." Meanwhile, he wrote:

> The primary objective of United States policy toward the Soviet Union is to convince Soviet leaders that it is in their interest to participate in a system of world cooperation, that there are no fundamental causes for war between our two nations, and that the security and prosperity of the

Soviet Union ... is being jeopardized by the aggressive militaristic imperialism such as that in which the Soviet Union is now engaged.

Clifford was certain that the Russians were not interested in real cooperation in September 1946. He reviewed many of the agreements the Soviet Union had made with the United States during and just after the war. He found that the Soviets had broken most of them, some flagrantly, others very subtly. Had these agreements been adhered to, Clifford wrote, they "would have avoided practically all of the causes of disagreement existing between the two countries."

Not only did the Russians break agreements, Clifford wrote, they also behaved aggressively at almost every turn. The Red Army was being maintained at full strength after the war. It was being highly mechanized, and was "in a state of constant readiness for war and is placed strategically to move against any part of the Eurasian continent."* Intelligence reports indicated that the Soviets were making aircraft in German plants in their occupation zone. The Russians also took whatever naval vessels they could find, and refused to return American ships assigned to them under lend-lease. "German scientists have been kidnaped, former German pilots now working in the United States zone have been enticed into the Soviet zone, Soviet agents have illegally entered the American zone for the purpose of collecting documents on German atomic research, and German jet propulsion experts have been recruited through German intermediaries for service with the Soviets," Clifford wrote.

Clifford's evidence was the same as Kennan's, with the addition of fresh intelligence on Russian behavior after the war. Clifford's conclusion was similar to Kennan's, too: America had to be firm and unyielding. "In addition to maintaining our own strength, the United States should support and assist all democratic countries

* Years later these intelligence estimates were discredited. The Red Army was demobilizing, too, and was probably in no position to conduct offensive operations in Europe in late 1946.

which are in any way menaced or endangered by the U.S.S.R.,"
Clifford said. "Providing military support in case of attack is a last
resort; a more effective barrier to communism is strong economic
support." Finally, the Russians had to realize "that we are too
strong to be beaten and too determined to be frightened."

Clifford's memorandum remained a secret document until
September 1968, when Arthur Krock published it as an appendix
to his memoirs. It is clearly one of the most important documents
in modern America's diplomatic history. According to Clifford,
President Truman seized on the report enthusiastically. He had
just a few dozen copies printed, and locked them all up in a White
House safe. (Clifford himself never got a printed copy; a carbon of
the final draft is in his files today. There is no copy in the State
Department's files.) The memorandum came to Truman just when
he needed it most. He must have been hoping for this sort of
encompassing statement when he asked Clifford to undertake a
study of Soviet-American relations.

The memorandum was entirely consistent with the important
decisions Truman had made regarding Iran and the Dardanelles.
Yet it went further, offering policy guidelines for all occasions, not
merely justifications for particular decisions. Clifford stated the
problem, its causes and a possible solution. He provided an
eloquent analysis. But he also caught the trend in official
American thinking. Few of the officials who contributed their
thoughts to his project would have disagreed with any important
section of the final draft. But it seems fair to speculate few others
had thought out the problems of Soviet-American relations so
thoroughly. No doubt Clifford's careful compilation of past Russian evasiveness and current Soviet aggressiveness was depressing.
But it was no more than everyone in official Washington believed
was accurate. Clifford merely compiled a complete record.

The coincidence of the Wallace speech and the Clifford
memorandum seems in retrospect to have marked a crucial turning point. After September 1946 there was no indecision in
American foreign policy, at least as it was presented by the

president and his associates. Wallace's departure from the cabinet ended the possibility of any compromise between his left wing of the Democratic party and Truman's center. Clifford's memorandum confirmed a hardening in the thinking of important American officials. Both Clifford and Dean Acheson recalled twenty years later that after that September, the Truman administration accepted the probability that the Soviet Union and its allies would form one bloc, hostile to the West, with which no meaningful understanding would be possible for years.

One can only speculate about the motives of Marshal Stalin and his colleagues at this time. Quite obviously, in the fall of 1946 the Soviet Union also felt that there was no possibility of a useful and permanent peace agreement with the Western powers. But had Stalin ever hoped for that kind of agreement? There is no good evidence that he had. Throughout the war Stalin suspected that Britain and the United States were keeping information from him and were making plans without consulting him. He was right. He undoubtedly thought the great similarity of Anglo-American views at Potsdam and Yalta were further proof of collusion against him. The creation of Bizonia must have provided additional confirmation. Stalin saw that Britain and the United States remained closely aligned at the United Nations, at the peace conferences, and in Allied counsels on the future of occupied Europe. And he knew that America had atomic weapons, and Russia did not.

No real common interest united the Big Three after Germany and Japan surrendered. Stalin never shared the Anglo-American view of an ideal postwar world, despite the Soviet Union's acceptance of loftily worded declarations of intent during and after the war. Stalin reverted to goals that Russian governments had pursued for centuries—access to the Mediterranean, control over the corridors by which European conquerors entered Russia, and stronger influence in the Near and Middle East.

Added to these was the crusading nature of Soviet Communism that had alienated Western nations before 1940, and did not disappear during the war. The wartime experience did nothing to overcome the mistrust that had grown in the Kremlin as a result of twenty years of mistreatment by the "established" nations of Europe and America. The Bolsheviks remained extremely suspicious of Western intentions.

Whether Stalin's ambitions were as grandiose as Washington's pessimists believed remains an historical puzzle. Hindsight suggests that Kennan and Clifford both overestimated the Soviet Union's capacities to conduct offensive political action around the world. It is also likely that Stalin realized the important difference, for example, between Poland and Hungary on one hand, and Italy and France on the other. In the former he enjoyed both clear interests and a free hand. But Western Europe was part of the Anglo-American sphere of influence, and the United States and Britain, Stalin must have realized, would react differently if Communism threatened their direct interests.

The important fact for this study is that in 1946 American (and British) officials perceived a general pattern of Soviet aggressiveness. Eastern Europe, Germany, Iran, Turkey, Greece, Yugoslavia, China—all were areas along the Soviet border, and all were the scene of ambitious Soviet or Communist initiatives during 1946. It may have been true, as future developments suggest, that these were really the outer limits of Stalin's interests, but could British or American officials have risked depending on that assumption in late 1946? No less an authority than Maxim Litvinov had told the United States that granting one set of Soviet demands would only lead to further demands. Subsequent events which now suggest that Stalin's ambitions were limited all occurred in the context of an active American policy of "containment."

From the American point of view, the situation in late 1946 was by no means hopeless. Accepting the likelihood of an "East-West split," as the press was calling it, did not preclude the possibility of making further progress, especially with peace treaties. In late September the Big Three agreed on procedures to accelerate the deliberations of the Paris Peace Conference to insure that it achieved something before adjourning.

The Russians were visibly anxious to avoid any direct confrontation with the United States or Britain. In late September, and again a month later, Stalin answered the questions of Western newsmen in the most conciliatory terms he had used all year. He told Alexander Werth of the *Manchester Guardian* and *London Sunday Times* that he did not believe "in a real danger of a 'new war,' " and that America's monopoly of atomic weapons was not a serious threat to peace. He even contradicted a propaganda line then common in the Soviet Press: "I do not think the ruling circles of Great Britain and the United States of America could create a 'capitalist encirclement' of the Soviet Union even if they wanted to do this, which, however, we cannot affirm."

In late October Stalin gave similar answers to questions posed by Hugh Baillie of the United Press. He said he did not agree that there were "increasing tensions between the U.S.S.R. and the U.S.A.," and expressed confidence that a peace treaty with Germany was possible. He described Russia's attitude to American warships in the Mediterranean as "an indifferent one," although Moscow Radio had been calling American naval movements "provocative" since August.

Such friendly gestures might have been welcomed enthusiastically in Washington several months earlier, but in the autumn of 1946 they were received skeptically. By then American officials mistrusted Stalin too fundamentally to be moved by his newspaper interviews. The administration had begun to explain publicly its problems in dealing with the Soviet Union. (Forrestal, among others, had recommended doing so at the time of the note on the Straits.) When asked for their views on Stalin's two statements, spokesmen for the administration were cautious and pessimistic, but they were not hostile.

It was in America's interest to preserve the *status quo*. The United States could not have unilaterally initiated a change in the relationship between Russia and the West during a congressional election campaign, and at a time when the president's authority was weak. Nor was the need for a dramatic new policy recognized that fall. Even when the elections were over and Truman's position had improved, America had to be persuaded by circumstance to undertake bold action; it could not act alone. Public opinion and political pressures created restrictive limits on the Truman administration's freedom to maneuver. The public, preoccupied with the meat crisis and other mundane discomforts, was as unprepared for new foreign initiatives as it had been the previous spring, when the American attitude first began to toughen appreciably. The principal issue in the Congress was how to reduce the national budget.

In Washington in late 1946—as in any capital at any time—there was a conventional wisdom about the world and its immediate future which encompassed the thoughts of most officials in the city. According to that conventional wisdom, world affairs were in a period of transition; where the transition might lead depended on the decisions of others. This feeling of impotence inevitably produced low morale. The stumblings of the president and the election of an apparently reactionary Congress disheartened both civil servants and appointed officials in Washington. One official has recalled, "We had no authority, no precedent, a weak president and a Republican Congress—what could we do?"*

From September 1946 onward, the United States was preparing to adapt to a new and ominous interpretation of Soviet policy. The Truman administration's position, public opinion and congressional attitudes were all changing. But none of them moved steadily in one direction. Men and statesmen both stumble along more often than they move boldly and inexorably ahead; so they did in the last months of 1946.

The news from abroad was contradictory. In Germany and Austria relations among the Big Three steadily deteriorated. The Berlin municipal elections in October and the Russian reaction to

_____

* The official was Joseph M. Jones, then a publicist in the State Department.

them symbolized the division over Germany. (Britain and the United States were then completing preparations for Bizonia.) In Austria the United States had begun to openly attack Soviet occupation policy, using U.S. Army newspapers in Vienna to do so. A bitter exchange continued throughout October.

Events in Eastern Europe were also discouraging. The Rumanian and Bulgarian elections, both of them obviously rigged, Britain's dispute with Albania over the Corfu Channel and the worsening Polish situation all foretold continuing bad relations between East and West.

But the situation at the Paris Peace Conference, it will be recalled, was much better. The conference made genuine progress, despite the bitter propaganda which typified most of the speeches of Soviet delegates and their allies. When the Council of Foreign Ministers convened in New York in early November 1946, to approve final drafts of the treaties with Germany's former satellites, both sides were optimistic. After some pointed discussions, the treaties were approved, and that optimism appeared to be justified. It was encouraged further when Molotov agreed to hold another foreign ministers' meeting in Moscow in March, and again two weeks later when the Soviet Union abstained in the vote on the Baruch Plan. The collapse of the Soviet-inspired government in Azerbaijan in December also improved the atmosphere. It was the first loss of territory for the Soviet Union after the war.

In Britain, the disheartening news from Central and Eastern Europe was ignored, and the good news from Paris and New York became the basis of a hopeful reevaluation of the world situation. The American press was also impressed by the novelty of so much good news at once, but the administration was not sanguine. Byrnes let it be known that he thought his own tough talk, not a change in Russian policy, had persuaded Molotov to agree to the five peace treaties. The State Department gave cautious briefings to correspondents on the meaning of these new developments.

According to Benjamin Cohen, an intimate associate, the general sense of optimism that was widespread at the end of 1946 did not affect Byrnes. His skepticism was evident when, after Moscow was chosen as the site of the next foreign ministers' meeting, he insisted that Molotov promise not to obstruct Western journalists who would report the meeting. Molotov made the promise, but American journalists were not convinced, and asked for reliable assurances that they would be as free to cover the meeting as they had all others.

It was the sort of topic Byrnes could have ignored if he had wanted to avoid any strain on Soviet-American relations. He knew this was a sensitive topic; Soviet authorities and Western reporters had never been friendly. (In November, Moscow correspondents of American radio networks had been told they could not use short-wave radio to transmit their reports, because the Soviet government needed all available channels.) Byrnes must have decided that the rights of American journalists and the necessity for publicizing the conference were more important than the appearance of friendly relations with Russia, which he thought were fundamentally bad anyhow.

This same tough attitude affected the administration's position on foreign aid in late 1946. During the war, aid to impoverished or devastated nations was regarded as an international responsibility. American interest had made possible the creation of UNRRA, the United Nations Relief and Rehabilitation Administration, in 1943, and for some time afterward the United States remained dedicated to the principle of multilateral aid. But UNRRA was not entirely successful. The United States contributed most of its funds, and its headquarters in Washington had the appearance and status of an American government agency. Reports of inefficient UNRRA administration were common. During 1945, there were indications that some UNRRA aid was being used for political purposes, especially by Tito's supporters in Yugoslavia, who had some control over the distribution of aid in their country. American enthusiasm for the UNRRA idea waned, both inside the government and among the public.

In late 1945 the United States decided that UNRRA should

complete its activities by the end of 1946. At the time, it was not a controversial decision. But 1946 was a year of famine in much of the world. Poverty continued to spread, and as UNRRA's life came to an end, many nations and individuals began to agitate for a continuation of the organization or an adequate successor to it. Fiorello H. LaGuardia, the former mayor of New York City who was then director general of UNRRA, proposed in November, 1946, that a $40,000,000 emergency food fund be established by the United Nations and financed by member nations. He criticized American policy as politically motivated, and protested that aid should be considered as relief to the needy people of the world, not gifts to governments. But LaGuardia was not speaking for the American government, which had other ideas.

The administration had decided that UNRRA was a liability, not sufficiently successful overseas and unpopular in Congress. In November 1945 the House of Representatives passed an amendment to the UNRRA appropriations bill for 1946 stipulating that no aid be given to countries that did not allow American journalists to report freely on its use. The amendment was a rebuke to several governments in Eastern Europe, all supported by the Russians. Never before had either house of Congress cast a vote so clearly motivated by anti-Soviet feelings. The Senate dropped the amendment in 1945, but passed it into law in July 1946, as part of another UNRRA appropriations bill.

Byrnes agreed with Congress that assistance should not be given to countries that exploited it for unfriendly political purposes. He cabled from Paris in September a suggestion that aid should be restricted to friendly countries like Turkey and Greece, and withheld from others which "from helplessness or otherwise are opposed to our principles." Byrnes was reacting to the propaganda about "dollar diplomacy" and "dollar imperialism" which was so often heard during the Paris Peace Conference.

A month later Byrnes decided impetuously to cancel aid to Czechoslovakia after the Czechs had enthusiastically applauded some gratuitous anti-American oratory. That decision encouraged

LaGuardia and others to question America's motives. Byrnes may have acted vindictively and hastily, but his inclination to withhold assistance from those who did not appreciate it was shared by most important members of the administration, including the president, and by Congress. Like Byrnes, Truman was an old-school politician who accepted the idea that politics involves both giving and taking, and that bargains require at least two parties. Both men felt unable to give vast amounts of money and food to governments that had nothing but hostile words for the United States, even if their people were hungry and destitute.

These political and emotional considerations had a negative effect on American foreign aid policy. An important difference remained between withholding aid from unfriendly nations and giving it to friendly and deserving ones in adequate amounts. The administration had decided, as Byrnes put it in November, "that whatever the United States does in the way of relief should be done by the United States unilaterally. We want to give aid as the United States and not as a member of an international organization."

But there had been no sign that America's unilateral aid would approach the level of its former contributions to UNRRA, which had been more than $1 billion in 1946. During the autumn the administration decided to ask Congress for $350 million to make up for the loss of UNRRA aid, but there was no plan to ask for any more as 1946 ended.

Many officials in the State Department thought this was inadequate. One was Loy Henderson in the Office of Middle Eastern and African Affairs, who tried several times during the year to get loans or grants approved for Turkey and Greece. "We were always told that Greece was too poor to repay a loan, and that Turkey was not an ally," Henderson has recalled.

Early in November, Forrestal asked Acheson (who was acting secretary) what U.S. policy was regarding aid to Turkey. Acheson replied that "the U.K. should furnish arms to Turkey and Greece." Acheson made plain the administration's desire to leave Britain in the dominant position in the Middle East. He told Forrestal that if Britain became unable to supply the necessary arms, America would give them to the British, who would transfer them to Turkey and Greece. The United States would extend credits not exceeding $10 million to Iran for the purchase of military equipment, but "no further exceptions to the current policy will be made unless essential to the American interest."

Although Byrnes had told Bevin that America would provide aid to Greece, Greek requests during the fall and winter were repeatedly ignored or set aside for further consideration. American officials told the Greeks that aid would not be offered until their government was broadened to include a greater variety of the country's politicians. The U.S. ambassador in Athens read a letter from Truman to King George VI in October in which the president said Greece was "of vital interest to the United States," and promised "substantial aid and supplies" if the Greek regime were made more representative.* The government was not significantly broadened, so Truman's promise was never tested.

In December, after several months of intense pressure from Athens, Truman agreed to send a special envoy to Greece to investigate the country's needs. He appointed Paul Porter, formerly the director of the O.P.A., to be his representative. Truman, the State Department and Porter himself** all knew that his mission was first of all a delaying tactic, not a prelude to significant new American aid.

Greece, Turkey and Iran, like every country which sought American dollars in 1946, had to compete with the priorities of domestic politics, and inevitably, they fared badly. The fact that all three countries were threatened by Soviet-supported Communists or Russia herself was not sufficient to overcome the strong tendency in Washington to reduce spending to a minimum. In the summer of 1946, Truman himself was first of all a budget-cutter. His special budget message in August revealed his priorities. The

* The quotation is taken from a Greek record of the encounter.
** Porter said this in an interview with the author.

president's inclination to cut the budget was mild by comparison to the attitude of the fervent new Congress elected in November. The Republicans intended to reduce government spending by as much as 20 or 30 percent.

If 1946 had been a better year for Truman, and if he had not been so thoroughly repudiated in the congressional elections, he might have thought in grander terms at the end of the year. His message to the king of Greece in October showed that the president was sometimes capable of a bold view of America's role. But he was erratic. At the same time he was trying to establish America's place in world affairs, he was trying to complete the reconversion to "normal life" in the United States. He had not yet realized that Americans would have to accept a new definition of "normalcy" if he was to achieve his international objectives.

Politicians and commentators everywhere agreed that the atomic bomb was the single most important factor in the postwar world. According to the conventional wisdom, as long as the United States had a monopoly of atomic weapons, the country was in no serious danger. Military men thought (or hoped) that the bomb could compensate for the large difference in size between the Soviet and American armies. Many politicians thought it allowed the United States to reduce defense expenditure to a very low level without endangering the nation's security. A few politicians, like Henry Wallace, thought that until the United States shared its atomic knowledge with the Soviet Union, the Russians would always be more afraid than friendly. In fact, the Soviets refused to be intimidated by America's bombs, and without intimidation, the weapon was useless—unless it was actually put to use. This option was never seriously entertained. Instead, American officials tried to find a way to outlaw the bomb or put it under effective international control.

The Baruch Plan for the international control of atomic energy, presented to the United Nations in June 1946, was the result of two years of planning and research in Washington. It was not hastily contrived. The plan proposed an International Atomic Development Authority to control atomic raw materials and production, and all research on atomic explosives. A system of international inspection would guarantee the authority's monopoly in these fields.

Once the authority was established and the inspection system operating, the United States would relinquish its stockpile of atomic weapons and foreswear their production. Once the plan was in effect, any violations would evoke "immediate, swift and sure punishment." Under Baruch's proposal, this punishment would be unavoidable, because the big powers' right to veto in the Security Council would not apply to atomic questions.

The Soviet Union produced counterproposals. As a first step, Moscow wanted all existing atomic weapons (*i.e.*, America's) destroyed and their production outlawed—before instituting any inspection system.

The U.N.'s Atomic Energy Commission, composed of twelve members, debated the Soviet and American proposals for the rest of 1946. America's allies, particularly Canada and Britain, tried to find grounds for compromises between the Soviet and American positions, but Baruch rejected their efforts, and the Russians refused to consider renouncing their veto on atomic questions.

In November the United States decided to press for a vote on its plan. Acheson had suggested that America try to encourage the commission to approve a report describing the differences between Russia and the others (all of whom, apart from Poland, already a Moscow ally, approved the Baruch plan), without forcing a formal Soviet vote against the U.S. proposals, thus allowing the Russians to reconsider their position later without embarrassment.

Baruch wanted a vote. The membership of the Atomic Energy Commission would change at the beginning of 1947, and he wanted something to show for six months of debate. Byrnes supported him, as did many influential members of Congress.

In the closing stages of debate in December, the United States might have altered its tactics to try to accommodate the Soviet position, particularly on the veto question. Some important members of the Truman administration had thought it was unnecessary to make such an issue over the veto, because any violator of the treaty would automatically be subject to punishment—war—with or without a veto. But Baruch and others, including Byrnes, thought it was important to exempt the treaty from the veto as a demonstration of its sanctity.

The Canadian, French and British members of the U.N. Atomic Energy Commission all tried to persuade Baruch to avoid the issue or modify his position to make it easier for the Russians to approve the commission's report to the Security Council, which was only a preliminary to the treaty anyhow. Baruch refused. In his last speech to the commission, he explained: "If the violators of a treaty can legally and without impunity escape the consequences of a violation of an agreement voluntarily entered into, then every treaty executed under the auspices of the United Nations contains the fatal defect that it is binding only so long as the major nations want it to be binding."

Baruch had decided that a fundamental principle of the United Nations—the need for unanimity of the powers—was a "fatal defect." No doubt, most of America agreed with him. In the same speech, Baruch said he could not recommend a treaty to the Senate which did not guarantee the punishment of violators. Nor, in all likelihood, would the Senate have approved one, as Senator Vandenberg wrote Baruch in an open letter in late December. By making an issue of the veto, Baruch had made it impossible to compromise his position, even by changing its appearance and not its substance.

He seemed vindicated on December 20, when the commission approved the report to the council based on the American plan by ten votes to none, with two abstentions—the Soviet Union and Poland. But the abstentions were much more important than they appeared at the time. Within two months, the Soviet Union had rejected all of Baruch's significant proposals, and perhaps the best single chance to control atomic weapons was lost.

The Truman administration was getting tough. The dream of a truly satisfactory peace was dead. In mid-December, U.S. officials in Germany let it be known that Russian-language broadcasts providing an American view of world affairs would soon be transmitted to the Soviet Union from Munich. But at the end of 1946, America was still not prepared to lead an anti-Russian or anti-Communist crusade. In October the War Department had announced that conscription would be waived at least for the rest of 1946, certainly not a crusading gesture. Some political commentators in Washington thought that the Selective Service Act, which authorized the draft, would be allowed to lapse when it expired in March 1947.

Throughout the autumn and early winter, the administration prepared a new budget which included reductions in government spending in virtually all sectors, including foreign assistance and national defense. Even this budget, when presented to the new Republican Congress in January, was received as a "shocking disappointment" full of "fat and watered estimates." The Republicans, with the support of public opinion, had every intention of cutting it further.*

Truman's State of the Union address of January 6 included no reference to a new American policy toward Russia. The president said that "the delay in arriving at the first peace settlement is due

---

* The idea (advanced by some revisionist historians) that the United States came out of the war with a consistent plan to create an anti-Communist sphere of influence in Western Europe—to secure markets for American business, or for any other reason—does not survive even a cursory examination of the domestic politics of 1945–47. The Truman administration never sought, and Congress gave no hint of ever accepting, the kind of military and economic aid to Europe that such a plan would have required. The politics of that period imposed austerity in government spending, most of all in spending on defense and expenditures overseas. Some American officials understood that this was a shortsighted attitude, but their realizations hardly amounted to a government plan to save Europe from Communism.

partly to the difficulty of reaching an agreement with the Soviet Union on the terms of settlement." But this "should not be allowed to obscure the fact that the basic interests of both nations [Russia and America] lie in the early making of a peace under which the peoples of all countries may return . . . to the essential tasks of production and reconstruction." Truman also said that "strength on the part of the peace-loving nations is still the greatest deterrent to aggression," but four days later he announced a military budget $3.4 billion lower than the previous year's.

American decisions on China in December and January were indicative of the mood of those months—and evidence that the threat of communism was not enough to change American policy. Since late 1945 General George C. Marshall had been in China as Truman's special representative, trying to bring the Kuomintang of Chiang Kai-shek and the Communist Party together in one government. At first, he appeared to have great success. When he returned to Washington for consultations in March 1946, there seemed an excellent possibility that his mission would achieve its goal. But neither faction respected the agreements reached with Marshall early in the year.

After he returned from Washington, the situation deteriorated steadily. Serious fighting between the Kuomintang and Mao Tse-Tung's communists broke out in several parts of the country. By July Truman decided that Chiang was less than honest in his dealings with Marshall and the United States. The President sent Chiang a long note in August, warning him that America was deeply disturbed by the Kuomintang's repression of liberal opposition and its uncompromising attitude toward the Communists. "Unless convincing proof is shortly forthcoming that genuine progress is made [sic] toward a peaceful settlement of China's internal problems," Truman wrote, "it must be expected that American opinion will not continue in its generous attitude toward your nation."

The note did no good. In October Marshall wrote the president that his mission had outlived its usefulness. Chiang learned of

Marshall's pessimism and made one last small compromise which Marshall agreed to play out to its conclusion, but to no avail. A final effort by a group of Chinese to mediate the dispute also failed. In December Marshall again recommended that he should be recalled. On January 3 the president ordered him to return to Washington.

It was obvious when Marshall left China that the United States had failed to unite the country. On January 29 the State Department announced that America would make no further attempts at mediation. Although American experts in China thought there was a reasonable chance that the Communists would defeat the Kuomintang in a civil war, the United States was willingly abandoning Chiang. The administration believed that the two factions could have been united in one government. The United States also believed that Chiang had been at least as responsible as the Communists for the failure of Marshall's mission. Truman knew he could do no more than give Chiang military and economic aid; there was no possibility that American opinion would support any deeper involvement in China's civil war. That the "enemy" were Communists made no difference.

Even before Marshall arrived home, Truman appointed him secretary of state to succeed Byrnes, who resigned early in January. Byrnes had been secretary for 562 days; he had spent 350 of them at international conferences, almost all outside the United States. Marshall assumed his new position at a relatively calm time. Violence in Palestine and the Polish elections were the major events of his first month at the State Department. The failure of the foreign ministers' deputies in Paris and the Allied Control Commission in Berlin to make progress on the preliminaries for a treaty with Germany were disappointing, but not surprising.

On February 4 Truman wrote a friendly letter to Byrnes, asking if he would make a "hard-boiled" speech on foreign affairs at Westminster College in Fulton, Missouri, where Churchill had spoken ten months earlier. This was perhaps the clearest sign until then that the president had given up all hope of a meaningful settlement with the Russians. A "hard-boiled" speech from the recently resigned secretary of state on the site of Churchill's famous declaration would not have been misinterpreted. Byrnes agreed to make the speech, and arranged to visit Fulton in April. But he later decided that he might interfere with Marshall's work at the Moscow meeting of the Council of Foreign Ministers, and the project was abandoned.

By the time Truman wrote to Byrnes, the optimism so obvious in late December in Britain and, to a lesser extent, in America, had disappeared. Difficulties with the Russians continued. Molotov's promise that Western journalists would have complete freedom to report the March meeting of foreign ministers was modified. Although the Russians promised not to censor any dispatches from the meeting, they announced that just fifteen to twenty American reporters would be allowed to cover the event. (Eventually, the United States delegation was reduced in size from one hundred to eighty-four, and the Soviet Union allowed sixteen reporters to take the place of the diplomats left at home. Thirty-six American newsmen covered the meeting.)

In a note delivered on February 14, the Soviet Union opened a new dispute. Russia complained that recent comments by Undersecretary Acheson on the nature of Soviet foreign policy revealed hostility toward the Soviet Union. On February 10, during testimony to the Senate committee that considered David Lilienthal's nomination to head the U.S. Atomic Energy Commission, Acheson had said, "I am quite aware of the fact that Russian foreign policy is an aggressive and expanding one." Marshall quickly replied to Molotov on the 17th, explaining that Acheson had to give an honest assessment, and asking him not to "attribute hostility to frankness." Marshall's note had no effect. Anti-American attacks in the Russian press and radio intensified markedly. On the 22nd, Moscow Radio broadcast Molotov's reply. He said Marshall's explanation "was not convincing," and Russia retained its view that Acheson's remark had been hostile.

The administration's attitude toward the Soviet Union was evolving systematically in an obvious direction, but the American public was less certain. After touring the Midwest in August 1946, James Reston wrote that Americans "have come out of the war with a greater fear of Russia than they ever felt for either the Germans or the Japanese." As Reston pointed out, it was a fear based on ignorance. Americans were afraid of Russia not because it seemed as menacing as Germany and Japan had, but because they could not understand the Soviet system or the ominous slogans of its communist ideology. In October an experienced pollster asked his sample a number of questions about Russian laws, customs, etc., and concluded on the basis of the ill-informed answers he received that "Russia is one of our largest areas of ignorance."

Public opinion was most easily aroused by events in Eastern Europe. Polish-Americans led a substantial number of immigrant Americans from Eastern Europe in public protests against Soviet policy in that part of the world. Opinion polls revealed that Americans expected the Soviet Union to try to dominate that region. Opinion on "the Russian question" was also influenced by the strong strain of "anti-Communism" that so many demagogic politicians had encouraged since 1919.

But these were not the only influences on American opinion. Important elements of the population wanted desperately to trust and cooperate with the Russians. Few Americans were prepared for the consequences of a confrontation between East and West. Optimism, an American affliction, could not be repressed.

According to the polls, Americans reacted strongly to specific events in 1946. For example, in October, after the Yugoslav and Turkish incidents, Dr. Gallup asked his sample, "Do you think Russia will cooperate with us in world affairs?" Then 32 percent said yes, 53 percent no. But in December, despite the administration's efforts to minimize the importance of the good news of that month, the same question was answered more hopefully. Forty-three percent thought the Soviet Union would cooperate,

40 percent thought not. Better-educated Americans were the most optimistic. Of college graduates questioned in December, 60 percent were hopeful, 33 percent were pessimistic.

Despite these ups and downs and the apparently high level of general frustration, Americans did not revert to isolationism. In Europe it was popular to interpret the 1946 congressional elections as a sign of an isolationist revival, but this was wrong. The country was frustrated by international affairs, but there was no strong popular sentiment to give up on the world entirely because it refused to follow the path America had chosen for it during the war. Opinion polls throughout 1946 confirmed this feeling. Dr. Gallup wrote after the November elections that the Republican victory "should in no way be interpreted as signifying a desire by the people to return to isolation." In a recent survey he had found "80 percent of the country opposed to pulling our troops out of Europe."

Americans seemed to be confident about their place in the international community. In November 1946, the Roper Poll asked: "If every other country in the world would elect representatives to a World Congress and let all problems between countries be decided by this Congress with a strict provision that all countries have to abide by the decisions whether they like them or not, would you be willing to have the United States go along on this?" More than 60 percent said yes, less than 20 percent said no. Roper would not have found such a magnanimous attitude in official Washington that November.

The distinction between opinion in Washington and opinion in the country became more important after the war. Postwar diplomacy—tense, complicated, even intricate—built a barrier between the American people and their government that will probably never be breached. Before World War II America's involvement in world affairs was relatively straightforward and usually easy to understand. It often involved little more than a choice between yes and no. Public opinion could and did influence such questions as whether or not to join the League of

Nations, or rearm in the late 1930s. Roosevelt maneuvered on his own to prepare the country for the war, but not until the shock of Pearl Harbor was the debate on entering the war resolved in his favor.

The war changed America's role, drawing the United States into much more sophisticated diplomacy. Suddenly Washington needed an opinion on a whole variety of arcane questions: Who should rule a province of Iran? Where should Italy's northern border lie? Which political parties in Poland were truly representative? and hundreds more. These issues could not be submitted to the general public; there wasn't time for such consultations, and even if there had been, what did the American public know about Polish politics?

So it happened that just as international affairs became more important for the United States, ordinary Americans lost much of their power to affect United States foreign policy. The "experts" in Washington began to assume that their special expertise put them beyond the influence of public opinion. A bewildered public was reluctant to challenge this assumption. A relatively small group of informed citizens in Washington—members of Congress, journalists and politicians—and an equally small body of academic experts and businessmen around the country became the administration's most important audience for foreign policy discussions. (This is still the case nearly thirty years later.) If these leaders of national opinion could be won over, the administration expected the rest of the country to follow them.

Informed opinion was not so erratic as public sentiment, but it, too, did not always keep up with the administration's thinking. In September, after August's confrontations with Yugoslavia and the Soviet Union, Reston reported from Washington, "The most striking fact in the capital today is that war talk is increasing while America's ability to wage war is decreasing." Yet as late as October, a committee of the American Council of Churches chaired by John Foster Dulles—soon to become a prominent hard-liner—published a pamphlet on the prospects of peace with Russia which recommended tolerance, cooperation and compromise. The committee suggested that America renounce "the acquisition of new military bases so far distant from the continental United States and so close to the Soviet Union that the offensive threat is both disproportionate to the defensive value to the United States and also incompatible with a policy designed to dissipate distrust and to increase good will."

The flow of discouraging news which eventually changed Dulles's mind was acting more quickly on some other prominent individuals. At the end of October, four well-known members of the Council of American-Soviet Friendship resigned, including Harold Ickes, FDR's former colleague, and Senator Leverett Saltonstall, a respected Republican. As 1946 ended, the stream of bad news from Germany, Eastern Europe and China seemed to remove many of the last justifications for optimism. The serious press devoted an increasing amount of space to news of communist incursions in all parts of the world. (Many less serious journals had been promoting anti-Soviet feeling since the end of the war.) In November, six long reports in *The New York Times* documented the communization of Yugoslavia. At the end of the year, a similar series of articles described the growth of Communism in South America. Daily reports from Poland left no doubt about the depressing course of events there.

December's good news, and a revival of optimism, didn't last. The Acheson incident, the Soviet Union's announced opposition to the Baruch plan (which it had appeared to approve in December), and the intensification of anti-American propaganda from Moscow all contributed to a reemerging gloom in February 1947.

The first eighteen months after the war created great emotional strains in the American body politic. The ups and downs, hopes and disappointments followed one after the other. By early 1947 optimism was—in the conventional Washington wisdom—out of fashion. Cynicism and "toughness" had supplanted it. The country at large in early 1947 was just beginning to reestablish contact with the "normalcy" it had sought so long, and foreign affairs were not at the center of attention.

The appointment of a new secretary of state on January 8, 1947, influenced opinion in Washington. Secretary Byrnes had come to the job as an accomplished politician, optimistic about his own ability to improve the international situation. Traveling to his first Council of Foreign Ministers meeting in September 1945, he told Anne O'Hare McCormick of *The New York Times* that it would take him "about three weeks" to make the Russians see some sense. That first meeting abruptly changed his mind, but he remained a headstrong secretary of state. Truman was always wary of him. (Byrnes's attitude was undoubtedly colored by the fact that he thought he should have been president himself.)°

Byrnes was not a popular or an influential figure in the administration or in the State Department, in part because he was out of the country so often, but also because he was unwilling to delegate authority. As a result, the State Department was not functioning smoothly when he left it.°°

When General George C. Marshall became secretary, he was a

° Byrnes thought he deserved and expected to get the vice presidential nomination in 1944, but Roosevelt chose Truman (who had gone to the Democratic convention prepared to nominate Byrnes).

Truman was not alone in thinking Byrnes was too independent. When FDR was looking for a new secretary of state in 1944 to succeed Cordell Hull, his close friend and aide Harry Hopkins opposed Byrnes on the ground that he was too strong a personality to "conform placidly to the role of a mere mouthpiece" for the president.

°° Byrnes's departure from the State Department remains something of a mystery. He had first offered his resignation in April 1946, and again in December because of ill health, but there are indications that his health had improved by the end of the year, and that he might have stayed on if the president had urged him to. According to Benjamin Cohen, an intimate colleague, Byrnes was surprised that Truman did not urge him to stay, and he was surprised at the speed with which Marshall was chosen to succeed him. In his own published recollections, however, Byrnes said Truman did ask him to stay on, but he declined.

Truman's feelings about Byrnes were complicated. The president wanted to be strong, and he may have feared Byrnes's similar ambition. Marshall, though a popular hero, was not a powerful politician, and was likely to obey instructions. One may fairly speculate whether Truman would have switched secretaries if his position had not improved so dramatically during November and December, and whether there would have been a Truman Doctrine or a "Byrnes Plan" if Byrnes had remained in office.

national hero and an experienced administrator. Truman had called him "the greatest living American," an accolade that the president seems truly to have believed. But Marshall did not have the ego of a politician. He was not constantly tempted (as Byrnes was) to assert himself. The new secretary would clearly be a powerful member of the administration who would enjoy strong support from the White House and almost everyone in Washington—and abroad as well. Even the leader of the British Labour party's left wing, Richard H.S. Crossman, had kind words for Marshall's appointment. "I cannot think of any other American who would command so much support in Britain," Crossman said. Marshall had been extremely popular on Capitol Hill as Army Chief of Staff during the war, and Congress was delighted with his appointment.

Arthur Krock, the conservative columnist in *The New York Times,* wrote soon after Marshall took office that he "has impressed persons who have talked with him lately as not only fully aware of the spreading poison being brewed by American-Soviet relations, but of its chemical consequences at home as well as abroad. . . . He is being represented," wrote Krock, "as believing that his supreme task is to try to persuade the Russians to trust what we say about . . . our peaceful plans. . . ."

The State Department welcomed its new chief enthusiastically. Not only did Marshall consult experts in the department, he relied heavily on them for advice. He encouraged his officials to settle as many questions as they could, leaving only the most important matters for his own consideration. He reestablished the orderly lines of command which Byrnes had allowed to lapse, and gave Acheson, his undersecretary, considerable new power.

A new secretary of state, new strength and self-confidence in the White House, important changes in popular opinion and the mood of Washington—all these factors, influenced by an international situation that remained ominous, made possible a fundamental change in the course of American foreign policy.

CHAPTER VI

"I believe that it must be the policy of the
United States to support free peoples who
are resisting attempted subjugation by
armed minorities or by outside pressures."
—Harry S Truman *addressing
the United States Congress,
March 12, 1947.*

On Friday, February 7, 1947, Minister of Fuel and Power
Emanuel Shinwell announced to the House of Commons
that "probably beginning on Monday," electricity in
most of Britain would be turned off between nine in the morning
and noon and between two and four in the afternoon. On Saturday, Shinwell gave a press conference, and said in a calm voice
that if the country did not cooperate with him to conserve electricity and coal, "we shall find ourselves in the next ten days in a
condition of complete disaster." The electricity went off on
schedule at nine on Monday morning. That night Prime Minister
Clement Attlee addressed his countrymen on the B.B.C.: "We
have come through greater emergencies in much more critical
times," he assured them. During the next week thousands of
factories closed. Unemployment rose quickly to more than two
million. Not until March 3 was electricity fully restored, and
normal conditions did not return for many weeks after that.

The fuel crisis brought Britain to the edge of a disaster. Had the
weather been just a little worse, the entire electricity grid might
have failed, reducing the country to chaos. By handling the affair

so clumsily the Labour government lost whatever good will it might have had. "In this short week," commented *The Observer* on February 16, "Mr. Attlee's government has suffered a decline in public esteem comparable to the melancholy experience of Mr. Truman's administration in 1946."

During one week of February 1947, the Attlee government made three irrevocable decisions about the most important international problems facing Britain in early 1947. On February 12, Bevin's final meetings with Arabs and Jews ended in failure, and on February 14, the Cabinet decided to refer the Palestine dispute to the United Nations. On February 20, Attlee announced that Britain would withdraw finally and completely from India by June 1948, regardless of how the country was then governed. And either that day or the next, the Treasury in London sent two notes to the American government via the British Embassy in Washington, informing the United States that after March 31 Britain would have to cease all aid to Greece and Turkey.

The decision to refer Palestine to the United Nations probably had nothing to do with the fuel crisis. Bevin's attempts to mediate had failed, yet the problem could not be ignored. The Cabinet decided to refer it to the United Nations to take some pressure off Britain temporarily; Bevin fully expected the United Nations to fail as he had, and send the problem back to Britain.

The fuel crisis may have had a greater influence on the decision to leave India. The idea of setting a date for Britain's withdrawal, thus forcing the Indians to try seriously to resolve their differences, had been considered for at least two months prior to February 20—since the meetings between Attlee, Jinnah and Nehru had collapsed in early December. Yet Attlee made no final decision throughout January or early February. During the fuel crisis Attlee devoted much of his time to the problems it created: the task of accumulating coal, reporting on the crisis to the nation, deliberating on regulations to enforce the conservation of fuel, exhorting the public to cooperate, and more. Yet while all of this was going on—and after delaying since December—the prime minister decided that the time had come to set India free.

Had a temporarily painful shortage of coal persuaded Attlee to act on such short notice? Surely not. Announcing an independence date fifteen months in the future was not a desperate decision, nor did it help relieve Britain's immediate difficulties. Attlee exploited the crisis to announce a decision he would have made eventually even if February had been sunny and mild. He knew that his announcement would bring protests that Britain was irresponsibly abdicating its obligations. He knew too that such protests would sound hollow when Britain seemed incapable of meeting any obligations.

At the time and afterward, it was tempting to explain the notes to America on Greece and Turkey as the same kind of clever strategem. Attlee himself said later, "By giving America notice at the right moment that we couldn't afford to stay and intended to pull out we made the Americans face up to the facts in the eastern Mediterranean."* The remark is misleading. By February 1947 the United States was fully aware of the facts in the eastern Mediterranean. But it was not aware of Britain's inability to cope with them. That was the import of the notice that Britain gave America on February 21. The most revealing evidence about those notes is the record British Chancellor of the Exchequer Hugh Dalton made of the decision to send them:

> ... I had for a long time been trying to put a stop to our endless dribble of British taxpayers' money to the Greeks. There had been great debate between the Treasury and the Foreign Office officials on the text of telegrams which I wanted sent to Norton, our man at Athens, and In-

---

* Attlee made this remark to Francis Williams, his press secretary and later a sympathetic chronicler of Attlee's government. But Attlee indicated that he understood the situation less than fully by adding the comment that "it wasn't ... until the Berlin airlift (in the summer of 1948) that American public opinion really wakened up to the facts." The vast majority of Americans had, in this context, "wakened up to the facts" by the end of 1947. The Berlin airlift probably made a stronger impression in Britain than in America.

verchapel, our ambassador at Washington. I had obstinately insisted that we would not pay any more after March 31 and that, if the Greeks wanted an army after that date, they must pay for it themselves. The Foreign Office officials had advised Bevin that this would be disastrous, and Norton had replied, arguing back on his instructions, that the Greek government would fall on even a whisper to this effect, and that no other government could be found.

Bevin, very short of breath because he had to walk up two flights of stairs ... since, with electricity cut off, the lifts were not working, tackled me about this and wanted me to come round to the Foreign Office and pore over a lot more papers. I said that I did not think I needed to trouble him with all this detail. I wanted firm instructions sent both to Norton and to Inverchapel, but I was quite prepared to do a deal and was willing that Norton should be allowed to hold his hand, provided we sent Inverchapel into action at Washington. Bevin said, not perhaps quite realizing what he was agreeing to, "Well, that's quite fair."

Most politicians find it difficult to make decisions. But in times of crisis decisions must seem necessary, if only to give the appearance that one is doing something about the crisis at hand. So crises provide excellent opportunities for taking action that has long been postponed. Dalton was right in thinking that Britain could not afford the aid it was giving to Greece and Turkey, but governments can live beyond their means for a long time. Bevin had procrastinated about Greece for months; but he certainly understood that Britain's relationship with Greece would have to change. It seems fair to speculate that the fuel crisis created the conditions which finally persuaded Bevin to act.

On February 20, a Thursday, Loy Henderson, Director of the U.S. State Department's Office of Near Eastern and African Affairs, drafted a top-secret memorandum titled "Crisis and Imminent Possibility of Collapse in Greece." Henderson based his memorandum on the reports of America's unusual collection of senior envoys then in Greece: Ambassador Lincoln MacVeagh,

Paul Porter, leader of the president's special economic mission, and Mark F. Ethridge, American representative on the U.N. Security Council's Border Commission then investigating accusations of outside interference in Greek affairs. Reports from these three men, Henderson wrote, "are unanimous in their alarm over the probability that Greece will be unable to maintain her independence."

Henderson continued:

> Greece is the only Balkan country remaining oriented toward the Western democracies. Unless urgent and immediate support is given to Greece, it seems probable that the Greek government will be overthrown, and a totalitarian regime of the extreme left will come to power.
>
> The capitulation of Greece to Soviet domination through lack of adequate support from the United States and Great Britain might eventually result in the loss of the whole Near and Middle East and northern Africa. It would consolidate the position of Communist minorities in many other countries where their aggressive tactics are seriously hampering the development of middle-of-the-road governments.

Henderson recommended that the United States should review her past policy of leaving Greek aid to the British, who could provide no additional help. He noted that "it was understood when the British loan was made last year that no further requests for direct loans to foreign governments would be asked of Congress."* But without a new American loan—which Congress would have to authorize—"the gravest consequences will ensue and the country [Greece] will be beyond our help." Henderson also suggested reconsideration of American reluctance to contribute to Britain's military aid program for Greece.

The next day, Friday, February 21, Dean Acheson read and

---

* There could be no better indication of the political mood of the postwar period in Washington. To get Congress to approve the British loan in 1946, the State Department seems to have promised—to Congress or to itself—never to ask for a similar appropriation for a foreign country again.

approved Henderson's memorandum. The undersecretary of state signed it himself and passed it on to the secretary, George C. Marshall. According to Acheson's memoirs, Marshall read the memorandum and "instructed me [Acheson] to prepare the necessary steps for sending economic and military aid" to Greece. Then Marshall left the office early to go to Princeton, New Jersey, where he was scheduled to make a speech.

After Marshall left, Lord Inverchapel, the British ambassador, telephoned to ask for an appointment to deliver two notes from London. Acheson took the call and decided not to disrupt the secretary's trip to Princeton. He suggested that the notes be delivered informally to be studied in the State Department over the weekend. They could be presented formally on Monday morning. Inverchapel agreed, and a member of his staff brought the two messages to Loy Henderson. Henderson immediately read them both.

The first began: "His Majesty's Government are giving most earnest and anxious consideration to the important problem that on strategic and political grounds, Greece and Turkey should not be allowed to fall under Soviet influence." It went on to review previous exchanges between Britain and the United States on this problem. The memorandum noted previous official expressions of America's willingness to help Greece. The British government estimated that merely to survive through 1947, Greece would need £40 million ($160 million) in economic aid and £20 to £30 million ($80 to $120 million) in military aid. More would be required in the future. But, the note concluded, "His Majesty's Government, in view of their own situation, find it impossible to grant further financial assistance to Greece" after March 31, 1947.

The second note was a similar analysis of the Turkish situation, concluding that the Turks could not both develop a strong economy and sufficiently strengthen their armed forces. Britain, the note said, could provide no more aid after March 31, though it could continue to send military advisors to Turkey.

These notes, Acheson wrote in an interoffice memorandum to

Secretary Marshall, raised "the most major decision with which we have been faced since the war." Would the United States accept the obligations Britain had decided to relinquish?

There were good reasons to think that it would. Secretary Marshall's coincidental decision to make preparations for unilateral American aid to Greece demonstrated that just the day before, there was a strong inclination inside the Truman administration to take that action. (Marshall had not consulted with the president or his colleagues at the time.) The United States had already shown its interest in Greece and Turkey. Byrnes had first told Bevin during the previous summer that the United States would like to help Greece. In October 1946 Truman had written the Greek king that his country was of vital interest to the United States. Turkey had received stronger assurances of American concern, particularly in the note to Moscow in August 1946, regarding the Black Sea Straits. In October Byrnes had told A.V. Alexander, Britain's new defense minister, that the United States would try to provide economic aid to Turkey.

Subsequently, several influential members of the Truman administration had decided that the United States would soon be compelled to assume many new obligations in Europe and beyond. One was Assistant Secretary of State for Economic Affairs Will L. Clayton, who visited Europe early in 1947 and wrote in a memorandum on his return that "the U.S. is faced with a worldwide challenge to human freedom. The only way to meet this challenge is by a vast new program of assistance given directly by the United States itself."

Clayton's phrase "human freedom" was a special codeword for one of Washington's preeminent concerns that winter: Soviet Communism. It was of no small account that the threat to Greece and Turkey came—in the opinion of the British and American governments—from the Soviet Union.

But there were other, contrary influences at work in Washington in February 1947. The strongest was the mood of the new Congress, which gave low priority to international problems. The

Republicans were committed to vast budget reductions, which they regarded as a panacea for the country's problems. Many of the people who elected this Congress apparently agreed with them. (Polls showed a national preoccupation with a balanced budget at the time.)

By late February 1947, the new Congress had already demonstrated a willingness to cut the military budget, which was more clearly related to national security than any foreign aid program. Yet Britain had said that a minimum of $240 million was needed at once in Greece alone. The administration had asked for only $350 million to replace UNRRA aid to five or six countries, including Greece. The president's message to Congress requesting this $350 million appropriation was presented on February 21, the same day Britain's two notes arrived. General Marshall would note the mood in his speech at Princeton on February 22: "Now that an immediate peril is not plainly visible, there is a national tendency to relax and to return to business as usual. Many of our people have become indifferent to what I might term the long-time dangers to the nation's security."

There was another, more subtle difficulty to be overcome if America was to assume Britain's burden in the Middle East. Congress and the public would have to be convinced that it was in America's own interest to take such an active part in events so far removed from the United States, and that the United States was not just helping the British government out of a difficult situation. Americans were wary of Britain after the war. Many suspected a revival of the British empire financed and defended by the United States. (Attlee's decision to quit India was, in this regard, excellent—and timely—public relations.)

Americans also had guilt feelings about Britain; they knew that the British had suffered more than they in the common cause, and they knew how hard life was in postwar Britain. A poll taken in August 1946 asked Americans, "Do you think the English government is trying to cooperate with the rest of the world as much as it can?" Just 30 percent said yes, 40 percent said no; the rest were uncertain.

Anti-British feeling was strongest inside the Republican party, and was closely identified with the reactionary right. Many Americans regarded the Mediterranean as Britain's corridor to its Asian empire. Britain's supremacy in the Middle East was an accepted fact, not least by the administration, which had encouraged the idea that Britain should maintain its prewar role in that area. These prejudices, which were strong in the Congress, would have to be overcome before the United States could agree to assume responsibility for Greece and Turkey.

The importance of the British notes struck Henderson as he read them. He showed them immediately to a colleague in the Office of European Affairs, and then to Acheson. The undersecretary also realized what Britain's decision could mean. He asked that a statement be written outlining the State Department's view of the new situation created by the notes. An informal committee, including Henderson, immediately began to draft such a statement. By midnight on February 21, they had agreed to a first draft. It was rewritten and revised the next day after consultations with the War and Navy departments. On Sunday, Henderson brought a polished draft to Acheson's home in Washington. He told the under secretary that he was dissatisfied with the way it read because it did not point in any direction. He wanted to be able to present a clear analysis and a definite recommendation to General Marshall on Monday morning. He could only do this if he could assume that America would take on Britain's commitments to Greece and Turkey. "Loy," Acheson said, "we're going to do it. You work on that basis."*

Like Henderson, Acheson felt that strictly on the merits of the two cases, the United States could not refuse. The Greek economy was in a shambles. Greece had lost many traditional markets in

---

* Acheson recalled this exchange in an interview with the author. He repeats its substance in his memoirs.

neighboring countries now controlled by communists. The Nazis had systematically debased the drachma, and no government action could revive confidence in it. The Greek treasury was constantly on the verge of exhausting its foreign currency reserves. A communist coup d'état seemed to be an imminent possibility. "I am convinced," Ambassador Ethridge cabled on February 17, "and conviction is shared by other members of the [U.N. Security Council] Commission that Soviets feel that Greece is a ripe plum ready to fall into their hands in a few weeks."

The situation in Turkey, though grave, was not so precarious. At the end of 1946 the American ambassador in Ankara had warned Washington that "Turkey will not be able to maintain indefinitely a defensive posture against the Soviet Union. The burden is too great for the nation's economy to carry very much longer." Walter Bedell Smith reported from Moscow in January that he had no doubt that the Soviet Union would continue to put pressure on the Turks, and that unless Britain and the United States gave plentiful long-term aid, "Turkey has little hope of independent survival."[*]

But Acheson's assurance to Henderson that "we're going to do it" was hardly the last word. How would America do it? There were numerous possibilities. The United States could agree to assume some of the burden in the Middle East, but insist that Britain continue to help, too. Or America could give Britain the money and material needed to protect the independence of Greece and Turkey without getting directly involved, and without doing any more than was absolutely necessary. Or a bolder commitment might be made. The British notes might be used as an opportunity to draw a line between the Soviet and Western spheres of influence.

The administration's final decision would depend on its answers to four questions: (1) Could the security of Greece and Turkey be

---

[*] This cable is quoted in President Truman's memoirs. It does not appear in the published volumes of U.S. diplomatic correspondence for 1947.

assured by many nations collectively, or were both countries dependent entirely on British and American generosity? (2) Was Britain incapable of stabilizing the Middle East or Europe? (3) Would American interests be served by a blunt and irrevocable declaration dividing East and West? (4) What could the administration safely ask of a Republican, budget-minded Congress and a nation anxious for peace, prosperity and quiet?

The first question had been answered by default before February 20—by default of the United Nations. The United States had lost confidence in the ability of the United Nations to keep peace. The administration thought it had failed every test, including the one in which America had put the most hope, the attempt to control atomic energy. In late 1945, as Truman recorded in his memoirs, the United States decided that "to refer the problem of atomic energy to the United Nations would give that organization a chance to prove itself." By February 1947, the Baruch Plan was dead, no successor was proposed, and as far as the Truman administration was concerned, the United Nations had proved ineffectual. The American government saw no possibility of protecting Greece and Turkey by a system of collective security, or of meeting their needs with multilateral aid. Both countries, it appeared, depended completely on their own resources and the aid of Britain and the United States.

Was Britain now truly unable to contribute? This was a crucial question in the days after February 21. Coincidence played a large part in determining its answer.

The notes on Greece and Turkey were a result of Britain's fuel crisis, and they were received as such in Washington. Since early January, the U.S. embassy in London had been reporting regularly on the serious plight of the British economy. These messages caused no great concern, but the fuel crisis had a much greater impact.

During February, Britain's deep freeze was one of the biggest news stories in America. On February 13, President Truman offered "everything within [this government's] power to relieve

the plight of the British people in their present fuel emergency."
The next day, Attlee declined an American offer to divert coal
ships then sailing to Europe to England's ports. The prime
minister was appreciative, but self-effacing. "The need for coal in
Europe is no less pressing, and we could not ask that cargoes
should be diverted from Europe to the United Kingdom," he said.
Attlee's attitude surprised the United States, which was receiving
increasingly alarming reports about Britain's situation. (In fact,
because the fuel crisis was equally a transportation crisis,
American coal unloaded at British docks in mid-February could
not have relieved the immediate problems.)

The Attlee government's own pronouncements, especially the
"Economic Survey for 1947" published on February 21, contributed to American alarm. This document explained, "We have
not enough resources to do all that we want to do. We have barely
enough to do all that we *must* do." Its statistics showed how truly
appalling Britain's position was.

On Monday, February 24—the same day that Marshall and
Truman first learned of Britain's notes on Greece and Turkey—*The
New York Times* printed a story on the top of its front page which
must have startled official Washington. The story, from a correspondent in Sheffield, in England's industrial Midlands, began:
"Nothing but an early and profound change in the attitude of the
British people toward the problem of national survival can
prevent the present crisis from becoming a steady slide into conditions of poverty unknown in the western world in modern
times." The rest of the story justified this gloomy beginning. It
described Britain hopelessly divided by outdated industrial arguments; a Britain in which, had a Tory government been in
power during the crisis, "there would have been a revolution"—or
so the *Times*'s reporter had been told "by labor, government and
employer representatives" in Sheffield. It was an absurd story, but
credible in the United States, where there was a deep suspicion of
the Labour party's socialism, and its effect on Britain's economy.

The same day there was a Cabinet lunch at the White House.

Forrestal recorded in his diary a revealing exchange with Secretary Marshall just before lunch began:

> Marshall . . . told me that Bevin had called him yesterday to ask that he, Marshall, request the Russians for a postponement of the Moscow Conference to April 15 because the northern Russian ports were closed and he, Bevin, could not fly on account of his heart. . . . He [Marshall] recited this incident not so much for the facts concerned in it but because he considered it so remarkable that Bevin should have asked him to make the request of the Russians.

The gloomy news from Britain continued. On February 25 *The New York Times* printed a dispatch from Reuters' financial editor warning the world of the chaotic consequences of an economic collapse in Britain. On March 1, Senator Richard Russell of Georgia, a respected member of the Senate establishment, suggested in an interview that England, Wales, Scotland and Northern Ireland become new states of the American Union, and that King George VI resign his throne to run for a seat in the Senate. Russell admitted that his idea sounded fantastic. "Yet I predict that it will come in the years ahead."

The United States had not expected a sudden British evacuation from the Middle East.* When Byrnes discussed Greece with Bevin in December, the foreign secretary said Britain would continue to provide military aid, but hoped that America could give economic aid. "At no time," Byrnes wrote in 1947, "did he indicate that, regardless of conditions in Greece, Britain would withdraw its troops on March 31, 1947, or any other specific date." The fuel crisis changed the atmosphere. Although difficult to imagine, a rash British withdrawal was suddenly conceivable.

---

* In his biography of Bevin, Francis Williams writes that Marshall cabled London upon receiving the two notes asking if they represented a fundamental change in British policy. Bevin cabled back that they did not. Williams interprets Marshall's query as indicative of his surprise, but it seems to have been more of a precaution on the secretary's part. Though the United States was surprised by the suddenness of Britain's withdrawal, it was no surprise that the British wanted American help in Greece and Turkey. And Washington had received word from American diplomats abroad that the Treasury in London opposed extending aid to Greece after March. There is no record of this cable from Marshall in the

As Acheson later recalled, he and most others in the administration remembered a map of the world from their school days on which "so much was colored red"—so much was the British Empire. "One only slowly allows reality to enter the mind and alter preconceptions," Acheson observed. "After the war, it didn't occur to me that this wasn't going to be the British empire any more. Day by day, though, reality seeped into preconception." Nothing could have given that reality more emphasis than the fuel crisis.

Suspicion of Britain remained a powerful political force, and a principal concern of senior American officials. The State Department committee established under Loy Henderson to evaluate the British notes on Greece and Turkey produced a report which is most revealing in this regard. The first substantive section of this committee report—which was apparently the first document in President Truman's hands when he made his preliminary decisions on Greece and Turkey—was labeled "discussion." It began:

> The argument might be advanced that the British are not entirely sincere in presenting the proposals contained in these notes; that the world situation will compel them to continue to extend assistance to Turkey and Greece regardless of what we might or might not contribute; and that the notes have been presented with the idea of pushing the United States Government out in front in the Near East and of prevailing upon the United States to assume the financial and other economic burdens which might otherwise be borne primarily by Great Britain. It might also be suggested that Great Britain has already decided to change its basic policies toward the Soviet Union and is now planning, instead of continuing to try to resist Soviet pressure, to endeavor to come to terms with the Soviet Union on a basis involving respective spheres of influence in

American literature on the Truman Doctrine period. Williams (now Lord Francis-Williams) recalled in a letter to the author that he saw the cable "among Foreign Office material which used to come to me for information when I was at 10 Downing Street [when he was Attlee's public relations officer]." He also recalled discussing the telegram with Attlee and Bevin at the time.

various parts of the world, including Europe and the Near East, and the conclusion of a close military alliance extending perhaps beyond the framework of the United Nations. Persons following this line of reasoning might further argue that the notes have been sent in the belief that the United States will refuse to bear what the British government considers to be an appropriate share of the financial and economic burdens, and that this refusal would justify the British government, in the eyes of the British people and before the whole world, in making such a change of policy

This, it should be emphasized, was the *beginning* of the first important American analysis of the British notes announcing the end of aid to Greece and Turkey. The committee apparently raised this line of argument first because its members feared it would be the strongest argument used against the administration if it decided to supplant Britain in the Near East. This may seem far-fetched in an era when the name "Britain" is usually written without benefit of "Great," and the whole notion of an Anglo-Soviet deal behind the back of the United States sounds ludicrous. But 1947 was a different era, with a different political atmosphere.

The committee went on to say that after "carefully" examining the situation, its members "are inclined to believe" that this suspicious analysis of British motives was unjustified and incorrect—that Britain really was unable to give more aid. But if the United States failed to provide the assistance that Britain was forced to curtail, "The British government may well find that it will be compelled to approach the Soviet government in an effort to work out some arrangement which would have the effect of at least slowing up the Russian advance in the Middle East and elsewhere."

The Henderson committee report suggests the mood in Washington at the time. It cited two possible consequences if the United States refused to provide the assistance that Britain was withdrawing:

1) Greece and Turkey, without financial and other aid

from either the United States or Great Britain, may become Soviet puppets in the near future. Their loss to the Western world would undoubtedly be followed by further Soviet territorial and other gains in Europe and in the Near and Middle East. The resulting chaos would be accompanied by an immediate weakening of the strategic and economic position of the whole Western world, particularly of Great Britain, and the very security of the United States would be threatened.

2) The British government might decide that, in order to avert the immediate Soviet conquest of Greece it must come to an arrangement with the Soviet Union, including a military alliance and the setting up of spheres of influence. Such an arrangement would greatly strengthen the Soviet Union, would weaken Great Britain and would tend to isolate the United States. The restoration of spheres of influence would furthermore undermine the foundations of the United Nations.*

The committee also noted the complications that their recommendation to give U.S. aid would create.

We realize ... that great difficulties are involved since certain responsible officials of the Administration and members of Congress, as well as large sections of the general public, are not as yet fully cognizant of the seriousness of the situation and would not like for [sic] the United States to expend large sums of money in the Near East ...

A day or two after this report was prepared, the secretaries of War, Navy and State met to endorse and recommend it to Truman for adoption. These members of the Cabinet made only one significant change in Henderson's report. The original document said: "Halfway measures will not suffice and should not be attempted. They would result merely in the waste of American money and manpower." The three Cabinet members "disagreed

---

* This last intriguing sentence suggests that the Henderson committee, and the Cabinet officers who subsequently approved its report, saw the Truman Doctrine as a means of frustrating the evolution of spheres of influence.

with" this statement and struck it from the document sent on to Truman. They also noted "the general difficulty being encountered in obtaining necessary appropriations from Congress to back up U.S. world responsibilities."

On the same day, the president told Marshall and Acheson that he accepted the need for American action in Greece and Turkey. He approved "in principle" the State Department analysis quoted above. On February 27 Truman invited a group of congressional leaders to the White House to hear the administration's interpretation of the situation created by Britain's notes. What exactly occurred at this meeting is something of an historical puzzle. Dean Acheson has written and said more than once that Secretary Marshall opened the meeting with a dry review of the Greek and Turkish situations which left the congressmen unimpressed. According to Acheson's melodramatic account in his memoirs, he then "whispered to him [Marshall] a request to speak." It was, Acheson said, "my crisis. For a week I had nurtured it. These congressmen had no conception of what challenged them; it was my task to bring it home." By his own account, Acheson then gave a blood-curdling account of the impending possibility of a "Soviet breakthrough" that "might open three continents to Soviet penetration. . . . We and we alone were in a position to break up the play." By Acheson's own account, this statement overwhelmed all in the room. Senator Vandenberg, according to Acheson, told Truman that if he would speak out in the same sense, Congress would support him.

Good as Acheson's story is, there is unfortunately no independent corroboration of its accuracy. In his memoirs, Truman notes that he and Marshall spoke at this meeting. He does not mention Acheson. Senator Vandenberg's diary also noted Marshall's speech, especially a phrase which Vandenberg liked: "The choice is between acting with energy and losing by default." Vandenberg, too, failed to mention Acheson.

The phrase that Vandenberg liked appears in the text of a statement which—according to the State Department's files—

Marshall gave at that meeting. The implication of Acheson's memoirs is that Marshall failed to sufficiently alarm the assembled congressmen. "My distinguished chief . . . flubbed his opening statement," Acheson wrote. But the statement in the State Department's files which Marshall apparently read that day doesn't seem to be a flub. Nor did it lack for colorful and alarmist language. If Greece were allowed to dissolve into civil war, a Communist takeover there was "altogether probable;" this in turn would endanger countries to the east and west. "It is not alarmist to say that we are faced with the first crisis of a series which might extend Soviet domination to Europe, the Middle East and Asia," Marshall said.

The secretary made another revealing comment to the congressmen: "Improved relations and better understanding with the Soviet Union will be much more difficult of achievement if we allow the situation in Greece and Turkey to deteriorate." In other words, Marshall wanted to improve relations with the Russians by standing up to them.

Whoever carried the day, the result of that meeting at the White House is not disputed. None of the congressmen present questioned the need to help Greece. (Turkey was not dealt with in detail.) Truman had at least the support of Senator Vandenberg (probably the most important man in the Congress in this case) and other important leaders for a new aid program for Greece and perhaps Turkey.

In less than a week the administration had decided in principle to assume Britain's obligations in the Near East. (Acheson informed Lord Inverchapel of this decision in a twenty-five-minute meeting on March 2.) It remained to be decided how aid would be given, and how Truman would present the decision to Congress and the country. The preliminary agreement to supply aid would be meaningless if these most important supplementary problems were mishandled.

From the beginning, those involved believed that however far the administration decided to go, nothing could be more important than explaining the new policy to the public. Francis Russell, director of the State Department's office of public affairs, told his colleagues from the War and Navy departments on February 28: "Secretary Marshall takes the position that the world has arrived at a point in its history that has not been paralleled since ancient history." This sense of grandeur dominated the administration's public relations program.

That program began on the evening of February 27, when about twenty diplomatic correspondents gathered at the State Department for a briefing. State Department records suggest that Marshall gave the briefing; according to other reports apparently stemming from Acheson himself, Acheson talked to the press. In any event, this was the first of a series of similar briefings designed to prepare opinion in Washington, at least, for the remarkable developments soon to follow.

In this first briefing, Acheson (or Marshall) informed the correspondents that the administration would soon ask Congress to appropriate aid to save Greece from economic collapse. He told them that Britain would soon curtail its Greek aid program, and that the United States thought it was necessary to support Greece to maintain the strategic balance with the Soviet Union in Europe. He did not mention Turkey, because it was still not certain that Turkey would be included in the administration's request for aid.

Only the day before, Acheson had decided with Forrestal and Secretary of War Robert Patterson that the president should make a specific request for aid to certain named countries, and not seek a general appropriation. Truman agreed. There was a disagreement inside the administration about which countries should be mentioned in a specific request. Many officials wanted to mention only Greece. Henderson and others in the State Department had a "big fight" to include Turkey. Henderson also hoped that Iran would be added, but was unable to persuade his superiors. Others lobbied for China and Korea.

The dispute over which countries to mention was colored by

the general confusion about Britain's real strength (or weakness) and future plans. The secretaries of State, War and Navy agreed at an early meeting that the United States should "propose top secret negotiations with the British at a high level in regard to the whole situation with a view to ascertaining British capabilities and intentions."

A parallel argument inside the administration concerned tactics. It was quickly agreed that America had to avoid the appearance of standing in for Britain in the Middle East. American officials emphasized this to Greek diplomats in Washington in the first week after February 21. But there were two schools of thought about what positive stand the United States should take. One group favored a cautious statement mentioning only the countries to which aid would be given. The other wanted an "all-out" presentation of a new American commitment to nations unable to defend themselves against communist pressures.

The White House canvassed both suggestions in the early days of March. Truman himself had to leave Washington on March 2 for a trip to Mexico and Texas, and he did not return until the evening of March 6. While he was away, the debate on the nature of America's new policy continued. The cautious school argued that Congress and the public were not prepared for an "all-out" speech, that Greece was insufficient cause for such a statement, that America would be overcommitting itself by making one, and that the Moscow Conference, scheduled to begin March 15, should not be jeopardized.

They were all good arguments. In late January the Greek government had finally been broadened to include most non-Communist parties, but there was still good reason to wonder if a country as unstable and corrupt as Greece should be made a *cause célèbre*. There was no reason to be confident that Congress would respond to an "all-out" statement by appropriating the funds necessary to give it meaning. Congressional reluctance to approve the British loan was vividly remembered. And although the preliminary work for the Moscow meeting of foreign ministers had not been productive, it still might be foolish to assure the meeting's failure less than a week before it was scheduled to begin.

The contrary arguments were not so directly related to specific and immediate issues. Their adherents in the administration thought the time had come to clarify relations between America and the Soviet Union. Many officials thought that a balance had been struck with Russia in August as a result of the confrontations in Yugoslavia and the Black Sea Straits, and that it was vitally important to maintain it. They were prepared to declare America's intention to do so. A limited response to the British notes would only prolong the confused international situation. It might be some time before another opportunity as good as this one presented itself, and the next opportunity might easily be one that put the United States on the defensive. Now the initiative was there for the taking.

These two points of view appeared to justify a good argument, but in fact, those who counseled caution were at a distinct disadvantage. Britain's notes—and its fuel crisis—were uncannily timely. They jolted Washington. The coincidence of apparent collapse in both Britain and Greece—suiting as it did the anti-Soviet temper of that winter—proved to be a powerful combination. The coincidence appeared just as the president and his administration were beginning to appreciate and exploit their new self-confidence and political strength. The effect of all this —even at the time—was to create a general feeling that the United States had reached an historic juncture. The mood in Washington left little room for caution.

On March 4 Secretary Marshall released the text of a Greek request for aid which, he said, had been received the day before. The Greek government had listed the many measures that would be necessary "for Greece to survive," but said there were no resources available to finance them. The Greek people intended "to do all in their power to restore Greece as a self-supporting, self-respecting democracy," but they could do nothing without aid and "expert assistance"—*i.e.*, American advice. The message did not mention Britain or the communist rebels which threatened the government.

Not surprisingly, it suited the administration's desire that aid to Greece appear to be an American affair which America could control; Loy Henderson had written the Greek request on February 28. He wrote a similar document for the Turkish government soon afterward. On March 4 Marshall commented that the situation created by Greece's predicament was "of primary importance for the United States." He said, "The problems involved are so far reaching and of such transcendant importance that any announcement relating to them would properly come only from the president himself. . . ." The next day Marshall left for Moscow. Before departing he told Acheson that the statement of America's new policy should be written without regard to the effect it might have on the foreign ministers' meeting.

Marshall's foreboding words were undoubtedly chosen carefully. Since the first briefing for the press, members of the administration had missed no opportunity to spread the idea that the United States was about to make a truly momentous decision. It was a tribute to their efforts that Washington caught on quickly. But preparing public opinion for an announcement of this kind was not necessarily enough. The unavoidable fact was that aid to Greece and Turkey would be expensive. The administration feared that the parsimonious new Congress might accept the spirit of a new policy without providing its substance.

The administration received coincidental support in early March from former president Herbert Hoover, just returned from a tour of Europe. Truman had sent Hoover to investigate the needs of Germany, Austria and other countries. He returned home with a startling series of proposals for Germany and Austria which would cost the United States more than $500 million in the subsequent fifteen months. Testifying before a committee of the House of Representatives on March 1, Hoover said that the United

States could expect requests for aid totaling $1.2 to $1.5 billion dollars before the end of 1948. Such high numbers upset many members of his own Republican party. Hoover's comments also contributed to the atmosphere of impending crisis which helped the administration when its program for aid to Greece and Turkey was introduced.

Staff work on the new statement of policy continued at the State Department. Truman had rejected an early draft because, in his words, it was "filled with all sorts of background data and statistical figures about Greece" and sounded "like an investment prospectus." He returned it to the State Department with a request "for more emphasis on a declaration of general policy." On March 5 Acheson appointed a committee to study the economic situation in the world's most important countries, and to suggest what American aid they might require in the future. This was the study which Forrestal, Acheson and Patterson had agreed was necessary a week before. The committee's findings became a basic document in the preparation of the Marshall plan several months later. By March 6, a new, strongly worded draft had been reworked several times.*

On March 7, Truman's first full day back in Washington, the president met with Acheson, Clark M. Clifford, the Secretary of the Treasury, and Admiral William D. Leahy, the president's military chief of staff. According to Acheson's record of this session, "the president reached the conclusion that he had no choice but to go forward with the program [of aid for Greece and Turkey]." He then called a full cabinet meeting.

Secretary of the Navy Forrestal recorded in his diary that the president "went into lengthy discussion on the Greek question. He

---

* The draft was too strong for some, notably George Kennan, who had returned from Moscow and was then posted at the War College. He read the State Department's draft on March 6, and found it very unsatisfactory, according to Joseph M. Jones in *The Fifteen Weeks*, an insider's view of the Truman Doctrine and Marshall Plan periods. According to Jones, Kennan warned that the Soviet Union might reply to such a harsh statement by declaring war. He recommended a less sweeping statement concentrating on Greece's specific needs, but—as Kennan notes in his own memoirs—his views were not shared by enough others, and his proposal was rejected.

said that he was faced with a decision more serious than had ever confronted any president; that he wanted to have the facts put forth before the Cabinet, have a full discussion of them, and then talk ways and means of procedure."

A long discussion ensued. "The general consensus of the Cabinet," Forrestal wrote, "was that we should support Greece to the extent that we can persuade Congress and the country of the necessity." Several members of the Cabinet still had misgivings about the government in Greece, and emphasized that further reforms were necessary. Secretary of Labor Lewis B. Schwellenbach expressed the opinion that by aiding Greece and Turkey, the administration would "again" be accused of "pulling British chestnuts out of the fire."

According to notes on this Cabinet meeting made by Secretary of War Patterson, Acheson did much of the talking. He

> made a general presentation of the case [Patterson wrote] showing the movements of Soviet aggression in the Middle East, evidently with the aim of isolating Turkey and thereafter gaining the Dardanelles and other Turkish regions. . . . Mr. Acheson also pointed out that the picture should be seen as a whole; that if Greece fell within the Russian orbit, not only Turkey would be affected but also Italy, France and the whole of western Europe.

Truman specifically solicited the views of all present. In the end the Cabinet gave him unanimous support for his decision to ask Congress to provide aid. The Cabinet talked at length about the best method of presenting the new policy to the country. Truman appointed a committee to discuss this question; it met the next day and recommended that the president address a joint session of Congress.

Also on March 7 the White House announced that a Caribbean cruise which the president was due to begin the next day had been postponed "indefinitely."

On Monday, March 10, the president met again with congressional leaders. Truman did "most of the talking," apparently

outlining his intentions in general terms. Senator Vandenberg said
the president would have to make a very frank statement if he
wanted congressional support.* At lunch with the Cabinet, the
president said that he planned to make "a very explicit statement
on Turkey and Greece" two days later.

Truman addressed a joint session of Congress in the chamber of
the House of Representatives at 1 P.M., March 12. His speech
began:

> The gravity of the situation which confronts the world
> today necessitates my appearance before a joint session of
> the Congress.
>
> The foreign policy and the national security of this country
> are involved.
>
> One aspect of the present situation, which I wish to present
> to you at this time for your consideration and decision,
> concerns Greece and Turkey.

The president continued with a review of Greece's economic
condition, and its request for American aid. He mentioned the
political problems facing Greece. He admitted that the Greek
government "was not perfect," but it was democratic, and its
faults were visible and could be "pointed out and corrected."
Greece had asked the United States for assistance, and "the United States must supply that assistance." The future of Turkey was
equally important, and although the Turks were in a better position than Greece, they too required aid which America would
have to provide.

"I am aware of the broad implications involved if the United
States extends assistance to Greece and Turkey," Truman said,
and he wanted to discuss those implications:

---

* One man at the March 10 meeting who had not been present when Truman met
congressional leaders on February 27 was Sen. Robert A. Taft, the chairman of the
Republican Policy Committee in the Senate and the leader of the party's conservative
wing. When Taft was not invited to the first meeting, Vandenberg wrote the president to
"respectfully suggest" that Taft be asked to any similar gathering in the future. This may
have been Truman's most serious tactical error from February 21 to March 12.

At the present moment in world history nearly every nation must choose between alternative ways of life. The choice is too often not a free one.

One way of life is based upon the will of the majority, and is distinguished by free institutions, representative government, free elections, guarantees of individual liberty, freedom of speech and religion, and freedom from political oppression.

The second way of life is based upon the will of the minority forcibly imposed on the majority. It relies upon terror and oppression, a controlled press and radio, fixed elections and the suppression of personal freedoms.

I believe that it must be the policy of the United States to support free peoples who are resisting attempted subjugation by armed minorities or by outside pressures.

I believe that we must assist free peoples to work out their own destinies in their own way.

I believe that our help should be primarily through economic and financial aid which is essential to economic stability and orderly political processes.

The president put Greece and Turkey into this broader context. He said the fall of either would be a great blow to the Middle East and to Europe, for both strategic and psychological reasons. "Should we fail to aid Greece and Turkey in this fateful hour, the effect will be far reaching to the West as well as to the East," Truman said. He asked Congress to appropriate $400 million for aid to the two countries through June 1948, and for authorization to send American civilians and soldiers to administer it. He concluded:

The free peoples of the world look to us for support in maintaining their freedom.

If we falter in our leadership, we may endanger the peace of the world—and we shall surely endanger the welfare of our own nation.

Great responsibilities have been placed upon us by the swift movement of events.

I am confident that the Congress will face these responsibilities squarely.

Not until two days after Truman's speech did Hugh Dalton record in his diary the story of Bevin's agreement to send the notes on Greece and Turkey to Washington on February 21. Dalton had no idea of the implications of those notes—"my little push for a small economy in Whitehall," he called his insistence on withdrawing from Greece. Only after Truman made his speech did the chancellor recall the encounter with Bevin three weeks before.

The sense of history which pervaded Washington from February 21 to March 12 was evident in London only for a day or two, when the House of Commons debated Attlee's announcement of independence for India, and Britain considered the end of the Asian empire. There was no indication in London that a fundamental change in East-West relations was about to occur. Stories from Washington in the British press gave a hint of the activity there, and newspaper readers learned of the "full funereal treatment" Britain was getting in America as a result of the fuel crisis, but nothing more.*

Britain might have paid closer attention to what was happening in the United States if it had not been so busy a time at home. The fuel crisis was not over when Bevin agreed to send the notes on Greece and Turkey; it did not end until March 3. The strain was immense and many ministers did not stand up well under it. Bevin's health was very poor, as his telephone call to Marshall suggesting a postponement of the Moscow conference indicated.

---

* The New York correspondent of the *London Daily Mail* wrote that "The pallbearers and morticians, masquerading as foreign correspondents in London, are making American flesh creep."

"It is quite on the cards," Dalton wrote of Bevin's coming trip to Moscow, "that he will collapse completely. . . ."

Bevin was well enough to make a statement on Palestine to the House of Commons on February 25, but his health may have been an important cause of the intemperate outburst against Truman which that statement included. His ill-considered recollection of Truman's Yom Kippur statement asking for 100,000 immigration permits to Palestine was revealing in another sense. It showed that Bevin felt no need to court American favor, although it was less than a week since he had agreed to ask the United States to replace Britain in Greece and Turkey. Even under terrible strain, it is hard to imagine that Bevin would have made the remarks he did if he had thought that it was vitally important not to aggravate the United States. In fact, the notes on Greece and Turkey must have been only one of many topics in his mind, no more important than several others. Like Dalton, Bevin probably did not fully comprehend the implications of those notes.

Bevin was back in the House on February 27 to open a two-day debate on foreign affairs prior to leaving for Moscow. He reviewed the important world problems of the day, with one striking exception. In a long speech covering many subjects, Bevin did not once mention Greece. His prognostication for the Council of Foreign Ministers meeting was pessimistic: "I hope the country will not expect too much from us at the Moscow Conference. We have terrible difficulties to face. . . ." What Bevin failed to say *The Times* said for him:

> . . . The fact must be faced that he [Bevin] goes to this conference with weaker hands than to the last. . . . The degree of real and permanent decline in British strength implied in the domestic events of the last three weeks is no doubt being greatly overestimated abroad perhaps in the most friendly quarters as well as in those less so . . . [but] not until she convincingly reasserts her real strength will it be certain that foreign policy itself is not to become, as time passes, one of the luxuries Britain must do without.

Bevin left by train for Moscow on March 4. The journey took four days.

On March 5 and 6, Parliament debated Attlee's decision to quit India by June 1948. The debate was more poignant than eventful. The worst Churchill could say of the government's policy was that it abandoned earlier pledges, none of which was very explicit. The fantastic era of the British raj ended calmly in the House of Commons.

On March 12 Parliament was in the midst of a three-day debate on economic affairs. Truman's speech came as a surprise and, to many, a shock. The general reaction in the British press was favorable, but wary. The Foreign Office indicated satisfaction that America would aid Greece and Turkey, but there were many in "official circles" who were startled and a bit dismayed by the bluntness of the president's words.

Bevin and Attlee had hoped to bring America into Europe, and now America was coming, but this description of events was an oversimplification. Neither Britain's decision to withdraw from Greece and Turkey nor America's decision to help them was an isolated event. Britain's retreat was part—and a decisive part—of the process by which Britain lost her traditional place in the world. The Truman Doctrine was the step that finally committed America to an active role in European affairs. America's commitment was by design; Britain's withdrawal was not.

Britain's notes to the United States of February 21 became an irrevocable admission of impotence. For both countries, the most fundamental problem after the war was their relations with the Soviet Union. Yet by deciding to withdraw from Greece and Turkey, Britain gave America the opportunity to resolve that problem for both of them. In effect, that is what Truman did with his blunt distinction between the free nations and the unfree. He drew a line between East and West which Britain had to respect. If the United States could settle that most important issue without reference to Britain, was there any reason not to settle all issues in the same way? In some cases, there would be reason not to. But the Truman Doctrine established the general pattern for Anglo-American relations in the postwar era. It left Britain in a decidedly inferior position.

This was not what Bevin and Attlee intended. They expected to revive Britain's influence once the damage inflicted by war was repaired. Soon after Truman's speech, the senior civil servant in the Foreign Office told the Greek ambassador in London that Britain would return actively to the Near East as soon as temporary economic problems were solved. Perhaps this remark was made out of habit; British diplomats were not used to giving up commitments permanently. But they began to do just that in 1947, and they continued to do so for twenty years. Only slowly during that time did the British people and their leaders come to realize what was happening.

With his doctrine, Truman had cast an enormous net to catch two small fish. It was the "all-out" speech so many of his aides wanted—a vivid, even florid statement of American determination to deal resolutely with Soviet or Communist ambitions. Yet Truman asked Congress for only $400 million, a moderate amount compared (for example) to the $1.5 billion of American assistance which former President Hoover had talked about just twelve days before.

The president's tactics were excellent, even if his prose was exaggerated. Having decided that the United States would have to accept greater responsibilities in Europe and the Middle East than most Americans ever expected, he had to bring the country to the same realization. To do so he invoked the rhetoric of World War II, the popular fear of Communism and the specter of an impending confrontation between the free and the unfree. He put Congress in a corner: if it accepted his premises, how could it deny him the money he requested? And in the atmosphere of the time, his premises were not controversial: the peace did appear threatened by Soviet ambitions; Americans accepted their country's responsibility for trying to keep the peace. The new element in Truman's speech was its new definition of American responsibilities: he described them in heroic terms, but had the good political sense to define them modestly—$400 million. The reality was cheaper than the rhetoric implied—at least for the time being.

Of course there was an element of risk in the "all-out" approach, but the administration seemed to pay little attention to it. Marshall's statement two weeks before that a firm anti-Soviet stance in Greece and Turkey would improve relations with the Soviet Union apparently indicated the administration's view of the risks. Marshall, Truman and the others felt it was a much graver risk not to respond in Greece and Turkey than to respond provocatively. Truman disliked ambiguous situations, and no aspect of his presidency had been more ambiguous (or more troubling) than relations with Moscow. "The President was not one to fuss or hesitate," Acheson later recalled. And "there was never much gray" in his attitude toward most subjects, as Clark Clifford has put it. Truman wanted to make America's position clear, and he did.

Congress soon indicated that it was favorably disposed to the Truman Doctrine. There were complaints about its cost. "This knocks budget plans askew," as one Republican senator put it. But the strong opposition that many members of the administration expected never materialized. Senator Vandenberg caught the spirit of the moment in a letter to his constituents on the day of Truman's speech. "I can only say that I think the adventure is worth trying as an alternative to another 'Munich' and perhaps to another war," he wrote. There were also some complaints about pulling British chestnuts out of the fire, but they were few and feeble. Most congressmen understood that Britain was running out of chestnuts.

Before the British fuel crisis, Truman would have found it difficult to persuade Congress or the public that the United States had a compelling responsibility to aid Greece and Turkey. After Britain's "collapse," he had no trouble at all—it was much easier than his own advisors had expected. Britain's troubles also revealed that the strongest power in Western Europe was hardly strong at all. The image of a three-cornered postwar world suddenly looked a bit silly.

The American Senate approved aid for Greece and Turkey by 67-23 on April 22; in the House of Representatives the vote was 287-107, two weeks later.

Truman got what he wanted because of the overwhelming influence of a remarkable string of political coincidences. But his own conscious contribution to this brew—the ringing rhetoric of the March 12 speech—may have been its single most important ingredient. The speech exploited the widespread feeling in Washington that a truly historic moment was at hand. Truman unified numerous loose strands in Washington's thinking. He transformed the apparent Soviet menace, the British collapse, the Mediterranean crisis and his own administration's new sense of strength and purpose into a coherent, "historic" policy. All the pieces fit; they no longer constituted a puzzle.

Second-guessing political history is a dangerous business, but a few second guesses here seem justified. The Truman Doctrine depended on all the ingredients of this enormous coincidence. Six to twelve months earlier, the popular perception of the "Soviet threat" was too vague to justify a Truman Doctrine. Without a fuel crisis, the popular view of what was still called Great Britain would have made it difficult to justify American commitments in the Mediterranean. Had the British notes been delivered to Washington a few months earlier, the Truman administration would have been too weak and embattled to cope with them.

The coincidence was reinforced, of course, by America's instinctive suspicion of Communism, lately revived in the 1946 congressional campaign. The slogans of roughshod domestic anti-Communism created a sympathetic political climate for an anti-Soviet foreign policy. Many newspapers, politicians and other commentators were spreading the blackest fears about Soviet

Russia, and Stalin had few serious defenders in the United States. When Truman suggested that fears of Russia were justified, he was certain to get a sympathetic hearing in many sections of the population.

These popular sentiments would have been weaker—and could have been ignored—had they not been reinforced by more respectable judgments on the menace posed by Stalin's Russia. The weight of opinion among informed diplomats, politicians, and journalists in Washington in early 1947 precluded a policy of mollifying Soviet demands of the kind Henry Wallace proposed.

Senator Arthur Vandenberg alone—as chairman of the Senate Committee on Foreign Relations—would have frustrated any attempts at appeasement. Vandenberg did not consider himself an emotional anti-Communist; he had studied the matter, attended international conferences with the Russians after the war, weighed the issues in his own mind, and concluded that a tough policy was required. Inside the administration there was no inclination to dispute Vandenberg. Truman and his associates shared the mood of the times.

The only serious criticism of the president's speech concerned one omission. Truman had not mentioned a role for the United Nations, either in Greece and Turkey, or elsewhere. Senator Vandenberg, who held a special regard for the United Nations, complained that the United Nations should have been informed in advance of America's intention. He also thought the Soviet Union should have had an opportunity to veto relief to Greece and Turkey through the United Nations.

Vandenberg's criticism was widely repeated, in Britain as well as in the United States, and by the Soviet Union. Vandenberg had strong popular support; a Gallup Poll taken just after Truman's speech found that 56 percent of Americans opposed bypassing the United Nations entirely. The administration was forced to accept an amendment to its proposal for aid which required the United States to cease its aid programs for Greece and Turkey if

requested to do so by the Security Council, and if the Security
Council agreed to give both countries U.N. aid. It was a
meaningless concession, but revealing nevertheless.

Americans wanted the United Nations to work, in part because
they believed in the U.N. idea, but also because they did not want
the United States to act alone in the world. This was not isolationism. It was naiveté, the result of too many years of isolation,
and too much optimism. The administration had exhausted its
hopes for the United Nations in March 1947, but the American
public had not. The Truman Doctrine speech did not dispel their
hope, but it did dispel the dream that America could guide the
world without assuming unilateral obligations. "Grave responsibilities have been placed upon us by the swift movement of
events," Truman said. America believed him.

A second criticism the administration had to answer was that
the Truman Doctrine promised too much—that it seemed to offer
aid to any country threatened "by armed minorities or by outside
pressures." In congressional hearings on the legislation to grant
aid to Greece and Turkey, Acheson—the principal administration
spokesman—repeated often that this wasn't the case. Greece and
Turkey were the only countries to receive aid under this legislation, Acheson said. No one else could benefit from it.

Acheson recalled in his memoirs that Senator Tom Connally of
Texas, the ranking Democrat on the Senate Foreign Relations
Committee, helped him emphasize the point in this exchange:

> CONNALLY: This is not a pattern out of a tailor's shop to
> fit everybody in the world and every nation in the world,
> because the conditions in no two nations are identical. Is
> that not true?
>
> ACHESON: Yes, sir; that is true, and whether there are
> requests, of course, will be left to the future, but whatever
> they are, they have to be judged, as you say, according to
> the circumstances of each specific case.

Congressional interest in this point suggests the extent to which public opinion continued to restrict the Truman administration, even after the fiery rhetoric of the Truman Doctrine.

A month after Truman announced America's new foreign policy, Bernard Baruch, again a private citizen, addressed the state legislature of his native South Carolina. His speech was not memorable, save for one sentence: "Let us not be deceived—today we are in the midst of a cold war." The phrase was Herbert Bayard Swope's; this famous journalist had suggested it to Baruch a year earlier. It had seemed too harsh then, but now Baruch thought it was entirely accurate. Walter Lippmann noticed the phrase and used it in his column; it quickly became a cliché, adopted by most of the world's languages.

Very soon it was also a reality in international politics. In June the general principles of the Truman Doctrine were made tangible by Secretary Marshall in a speech at Harvard. Marshall said that

> before the United States Government can proceed much farther in its efforts to . . . help start the European world on its way to recovery, there must be some agreement among the countries of Europe as to the requirements of the situation and the part those countries themselves will take in order to give proper effect to whatever might be undertaken by this government . . . .

Obscured but still discernible in that tangled sentence was the basis of the Marshall Plan. Ernest Bevin seized on it immediately, and organized a European response to America's offer. In July the Soviet Union rejected the Marshall idea, and prevailed upon Czechoslovakia and Poland—both of which had previously accepted it—to do the same. The line Truman had drawn tentatively in March was made absolute by Stalin in July.

This is how the confrontation between the United States and the Soviet Union began. Until the Truman Doctrine the differences between the two were polemical; after the Truman

Doctrine they were tangible. Most important, the United States had accepted a new commitment to provide the resources and power that Britain could no longer provide, to maintain a stable balance of power in Europe and the Near East.

When Bernard Baruch first used the phrase "cold war," he was describing a political confrontation with military overtones—but not a crusade. The crusade came later. In time the words "cold war" would symbolize an emotional, often mindless confrontation of escalating rhetoric and escalating armed forces. Encouraged both by international events (the Communist coup d'état in Prague, the Berlin blockade) and the vicious virus of McCarthyism in domestic politics, Americans succumbed to their apparently permanent temptation to oversimplify the world around them.

As a result, Stalin's death in 1953—which should have been a momentous turning point—slipped by as nothing more than the first of numerous missed opportunities. American fanatacism prolonged and embittered the cold war. The United States' failure to perceive and respond to the nationalisms which divided the Communist world led eventually to Indochina, where all the clichés of the cold war crusade were tested, and found wanting.

The foolishness of the cold war crusade seems to have convinced some historians that its origins were as perverse as its ultimate consequences. This writer does not think so. This book has tried to show that the American decision to apply power and resources in Europe and the Near East to counteract Soviet power was a reasonably sensible and perfectly understandable political decision. It was not the consequence of conspiracy or perversity, or a secret desire to encourage a cold war. It was the result of politics—that strange amalgam of prejudice, perceptions, personalities, national ambition and fear, design and circumstance which keeps history moving.

ACKNOWLEDGEMENTS

Many people in Britain and the United States generously contributed their time and recollections to provide material for this book. I would like to thank especially these Americans for their help: the late Dean Acheson; Clark M. Clifford, President Truman's special assistant in 1946–47; Benjamin Cohen, then counsel to the State Department; W. Averell Harriman, ambassador to London and Secretary of Commerce in 1946–47; Loy W. Henderson, director of the State Department's Office of Near Eastern and African Affairs in those years; Paul Porter, President Truman's special envoy to Greece; James Reston of *The New York Times;* and Professor H. Bradford Westerfield of Yale University.

Also, these men in Britain: the late Earl Attlee; Sir John Balfour, senior minister in the British Embassy in Washington after the war; Richard H.S. Crossman, unofficial leader of the left wing of the Labour party at that time; Christopher Mayhew, Parliamentary Secretary in the Foreign Office during the period just prior to the Truman Doctrine; Lord Sherfield, who, as Roger Makins, also served in the British embassy in Washington after the war; Lord Shinwell, who, as Emanuel Shinwell, served as Minister of Fuel and Power in the first Attlee government; Sir John Wheeler-Bennett, the distinguished historian who was an aide to Ernest Bevin after the war; Lord Wigg, who, as George Wigg, was Shinwell's private secretary at the Ministry of Fuel and Power; and Lord Francis Williams, Attlee's press secretary at 10 Downing Street.

I would like to express special thanks to Michael Donelan of the London School of Economics, who originally suggested that I write this book, and provided wise counsel.

None of these people—and no member of my very helpful family—is in any way responsible for what I have written.

BIBLIOGRAPHY

DOCUMENTS AND
OFFICIAL PUBLICATIONS

Bernstein, Barton J., and Matusow, Allen J., eds. *The Truman Administration: A Documentary History.* New York, 1966.

Central Statistical Office. *Annual Abstract of Statistics, 1938–1949.* N. 87. London: Her Majesty's Stationery Office.

Dennett, Raymond, and Turner, Robert K., eds. *Documents on American Foreign Relations.* Vol. VIII. Princeton, 1948.

Department of Public Information of the United Nations. *Yearbook of the United Nations, 1946–1947.* Lake Success, New York, 1947.

Economic Survey for 1947, Command 7046. London: H.M. Stationery Office, 1947.

Economic Survey for 1948, Command 7344. London: H.M. Stationery Office, 1948.

Hansard, *House of Commons Debates,* Fifth Series. London.

Hillman, William. *Mr. President.* From personal papers of Harry S. Truman. New York, 1952.

Koenig, Louis W., ed. *The Truman Administration: Its Principles and Practice.* New York, 1956.

National Income and Expenditure of the United Kingdom, 1946–1948, Command 7649. London: H.M. Stationery Office, 1948.

Notter, Harley A., ed. *Post-War Foreign Policy Preparation.* Washington: Department of State, 1960.

A Statement on the Economic Conditions Affecting Relations between Employers and Workers, Command 7018. London: H.M. Stationery Office, 1947.

Statement Relating to Defense, Command 7042. London: H.M. Stationery Office, 1947.

Statistical Material Presented During the Washington Negotiations, Command 6707. London: H.M. Stationery Office, 1945.

Truman, Harry S., *Public Papers of the Presidents, 1946.* Washington: U.S. Government Printing Office, 1952.

United Kingdom Balance of Payments, 1946 and 1947, Command 7324. London: H.M. Stationery Office, 1948.

United Kingdom Balance of Payments, 1946 to 1950, Command 8065. London: H.M. Stationery Office, 1950.

U.S. Department of Commerce, *Statistical Abstract of the United States, 1947.* Washington: U.S. Government Printing Office, 1947.

U.S. Department of Commerce, *Statistical Abstract of the United States, 1948.* Washington: U.S. Government Printing Office, 1948.

U.S. Department of State, *Foreign Relations of the United States 1946.* Washington.

U.S. Department of State, *Foreign Relations of the United States 1947,* Washington.

U.S. Senate Committee on Foreign Relations, *Legislative History of the Truman Doctrine,* Washington, 1973.

U.S. Senate Committee of Foreign Relations and U.S. Department of State, *A Decade of American Foreign Policy, Basic Documents, 1941–1949.* Washington: U.S. Government Printing Office.

MEMOIRS

Acheson, Dean. *Present at the Creation,* New York, 1969.

Attlee, (Earl) Clement A. *As It Happened.* London, 1954.

Baruch, Bernard M. *The Public Years.* New York, 1960.

Byrnes, James F. *All in One Lifetime.* New York, 1958.

Byrnes, James F. *Speaking Frankly.* New York, 1947.

Churchill, Winston S. *The Second World War,* Vol. VI, *Triumph and Tragedy.* London, 1954.

Clay, (General) Lucius D. *Decision in Germany.* Garden City, N.Y., 1950.

Dalton, (Lord) Hugh. *High Tide and After.* Memoirs, 1945–1960. London, 1962.

Fyfe, David Patrick Maxwell (First Earl of Kilmuir). *Political Adventure.* London, 1964.

Kennan, George F. *Memoirs, 1925–1950.* Boston, 1967.

Kirpatrick, Ivone. *The Inner Circle.* London, 1959.

Leahy, William D. *I Was There.* New York, 1950.

Millis, Walter, ed. *The Forrestal Diaries.* New York, 1951.

Montgomery, Bernard. *Memoirs of Field-Marshal the Viscount Montgomery of Alamein.* London, 1958.

Morrison, (Lord) Herbert. *An Autobiography.* London, 1960.

Peterson, (Sir) Maurice. *Both Sides of the Curtain.* London, 1950.

Rendel, (Sir) George. *The Sword and the Olive.* London, 1957.

Smith, Walter Bedell. *My Three Years in Moscow.* New York, 1950.

Strang, (Lord) William. *Home and Abroad.* London, 1956.

Truman, Harry S. *Memoirs, Vol. I, Year of Decisions.* New York, 1955.

Truman, Harry S. *Memoirs, Vol. II, Years of Trial and Hope.* New York, 1956.

Vandenberg, Arthur H., Jr., ed. *The Private Papers of Senator Vandenberg.* Boston, 1952.

Welles, Sumner. *Seven Decisions That Shaped History.* New York, 1951.

Williams, Francis. *A Prime Minister Remembers.* London, 1961.

MONOGRAPHS

Allen, H.C. *Great Britain and the United States.* London, 1954.

Almond, Gabriel A. *The American People and Foreign Policy.* New York, 1950.

Alperovitz, Gar. *Cold War Essays.* New York, 1970.

Alperovitz, Gar. *Atomic Diplomacy: Hiroshima and Potsdam.* New York, 1965.

Balfour, Michael and Main, John. *Four-Power Control in Germany and Austria, 1945–1946.* London, 1956.

Bernstein, Barton J. *Politics and Policies of the Truman Administration.* Chicago, 1970.

Calvocoressi, Peter. *Survey of International Affairs, 1947–1948.* London, 1952.

Campbell, John C. *The United States in World Affairs, 1945–1947.* New York, 1947.

Cottrell, Leonard S., Jr., and Eberhart, Sylvia. *American Opinion in World Affairs.* Princeton, 1948.

Curry, George. *James F. Byrnes,* in Ferrell, Robert H., ed. *The American Secretaries of State and Their Diplomacy,* Vol. XIV. New York, 1965.

Daniels, Jonathan E. *The Man of Independence.* London, 1951.

Dennett, Raymond and Johnson, Joseph E., eds. *Negotiating with the Russians.* Boston, 1951.

Donelan, Michael. *The Ideas of American Foreign Policy.* London, 1963.

Donelly, Desmond. *Struggle for the World.* London, 1965.

Estorick, Eric. *Stafford Cripps.* London, 1949.

Fenton, John M. *In Your Opinion.* Boston, 1961.

Gaddis, John Lewis. *The United States and the Origins of the Cold War, 1941–1947.* New York, 1972.

Gardner, Lloyd C. *Architects of Illusion: Men and Ideals in American Foreign Policy, 1941–1949.* Chicago, 1970.

Gardner, Richard N. *Sterling-Dollar Diplomacy.* Oxford, 1956.

Goldman, Eric F. *The Crucial Decade.* New York, 1959.

Goodrich, Leland M. and Simons, Anne P. *The United Nations and the Maintenance of International Peace and Security.* Washington, 1955.

Gowing, Margaret. *Britain and Atomic Energy, 1939–1945.* London, 1964.

Grosser, Alfred. *La IVᵉ Republique et Sa Politique Exterieure.* Paris, 1961.

Hewlett, Richard G. and Anderson, Oscar E. *The New World, 1939–1946, a History of the United States Atomic Energy Commission.* University Park, Pennsylvania, 1962.

Hopkins, Harry. *The New Look.* London, 1963.

Horovitz, David. *The Free World Colossus.* New York, 1965.

International Studies Group of Brookings Institution, *Major Problems of the United States Foreign Policy, 1947.* Washington, 1947.

Jackson, J. Hampden. *The Post-War Decade.* London, 1955.

Jones, Joseph M. *The Fifteen Weeks.* New York, 1955.

LeFeber, Walter. *America, Russia and the Cold War, 1945-1967.* New York, 1967.

Maclaurin, John (pseud.). *The United Nations and Power Politics.* London, 1951.

McNeil, William H. *America, Britain and Russia, Their Cooperation and Conflict, 1941-1945.* London, 1953.

Markel, Lester et al. *Public Opinion and Foreign Policy.* New York, 1949.

Meehan, Eurene J. *The British Left Wing and Foreign Policy.* New Brunswick, New Jersey, 1960.

Opie, Redvers, and associates. *The Search for Peace Settlements.* Washington, 1951.

Payne, Robert. *General Marshall.* London, 1952.

Phillips, Cabell. *The Truman Presidency.* New York, 1966.

Sherwood, Robert E. *Roosevelt and Hopkins.* New York, 1948.

Sissons, Michael and French, Philip, eds. *Age of Austerity.* Middlesex, 1963.

Snyder, William P. *The Politics of Britain's Defense Policy, 1943-1962.* Columbus, Ohio, 1964.

Spanier, John W. *American Foreign Policy Since World War Two.* (second edition) London, 1962.

Stillman, Edmund and Pfaff, William. *The New Politics.* New York, 1961.

Strang, (Lord) William. *Britain in World Affairs.* New York, 1961.

Taylor, A.J.P. *English History, 1914-1945.* London, 1965.

Ulam, Adam B. *Expansion and Coexistence: The History of Soviet Foreign Policy 1917-1967.* New York, 1968.

Westerfield, H. Bradford. *Foreign Policy and Party Politics.* New Haven, 1955.

Williams, William Appleman. *The Tragedy of American Diplomacy.* New York, 1962.

Williams, Francis. *Ernest Bevin.* London, 1952.

Woodhouse, C.M. *British Foreign Policy Since the Second World War.* London, 1961.

Xydis, Stephen G. *Greece and the Great Powers, 1944-1947.* Thessaloniki, 1963.

ARTICLES AND PAMPHLETS

Bevin, Ernest. "Foreign Affairs," a speech at the Labour party
conference, June 12, 1946. London, 1946.

Chatham House Study Group. *British Security.* London, 1946.

Crossman, Richard H.S. "The Cold War," in *Planning for Freedom.*
London, 1965.

Foot, Michael, and Crossman, Richard H.S. *A Palestine Munich?* London, 1946.

Labour party, *Let Us Face the Future.* London, 1945.

Lowrey, Sidney, "The Peace Settlement in Eastern Europe," in Toynbee,
Philip and Veronica, eds. *The Realignment of Europe.* London,
1955.

Schlesinger, Arthur M. "Origins of the Cold War," in *Foreign Affairs*
XLVI, October 1967.

PERIODICALS

Keesing's Contemporary Archives, Vol. VI. London, Keesing's Publications.

National Opinion Research Center Reports 34 and 27. Denver, 1945.

Chicago Daily News

Christian Science Monitor

Daily Express

Daily Herald

Manchester Guardian

Newsweek

News Chronicle

New York Herald Tribune

Observer

The New York Times

The Times

The Yorkshire Post

UNPUBLISHED WORKS

Balfour, Sir John. *Memoirs.*
Trowbridge, Thomas R., III. *The 1919–1920 Red Scare.*

INDEX